of the 20th Century

Elizabeth Scofield & Peggy Zalamea

Schiffer® Publishing Ltd

4880 Lower Valley Road, Atglen, PA 19310 USA

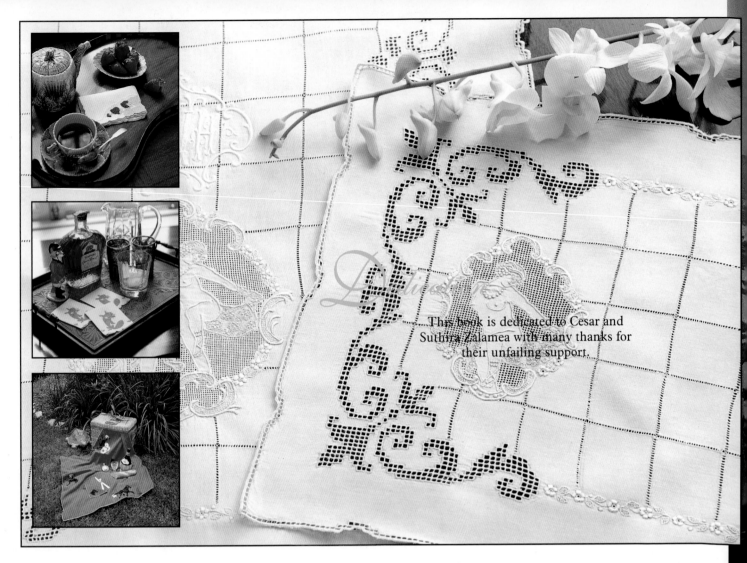

Dedication

This book is dedicated to Cesar and
Suthira Zalamea with many thanks for
their unfailing support.

Copyright © 2002 by Elizabeth Scofield and Peggy Zalamea
Library of Congress Control Number: 2002106916

Designed by Bonnie M. Hensley
Cover design by Bruce M. Waters
Type set in ShelleyVolante BT/Aldine 721 BT

ISBN: 0-7643-1599-4
Printed in China
1 2 3 4

Published by Schiffer Publishing Ltd.
4880 Lower Valley Road
Atglen, PA 19310
Phone: (610) 593-1777; Fax: (610) 593-2002
E-mail: Schifferbk@aol.com
Please visit our web site catalog at **www.schifferbooks.com**

In Europe, Schiffer books are distributed by Bushwood Books
6 Marksbury Avenue Kew Gardens
Surrey TW9 4JF England
Phone: 44 (0) 20-8392-8585; Fax: 44 (0) 20-8392-9876
E-mail: Bushwd@aol.com
Free postage in the UK. Europe: air mail at cost.

This book may be purchased from the publisher.
Include $3.95 for shipping. Please try your bookstore first.
We are always looking for people to write books on new and related subjects.
If you have an idea for a book please contact us at the above address.
You may write for a free catalog.

Acknowledgments

We wish to thank the following individuals for their contributions to our project:

Levida Allen, Country Elegance
Claire Beevers, stylist
Cloey Borden
Gregory Bruce
Anna Burns
Cooper-Hewitt National Design Museum
Phoebe Ann Erb
James C. Ford, Ph.D
Roslyn Golubock
Stan Gorski
Stephen Grout, Ed.D.
Keith Haines, Executive V. P., Aunt Martha's
Lisa Heller
Clara Prezio-Henry, stylist
Liana Howe
Annie Kapetanis
Paul Kerstetter
Richard King
Nicholas Koenig, photographer
Giles Kotcher
Lois Lowey
Remy Mason
J.J. Murphy
Dave A. Myers
Adelaida Ordoña
Paul J. Gutmann Library at Philadelphia University
Emma Picardo
Jack Rappaport
James Savoie
Masimichi Takeda, photographer
The Free Library of Philadelphia
Joseph Ugras, Ph.D
Peggy Yannas
Cesar and Suthira Zalamea
Princess Roo (a Rottweiler), champion couch potato
Ch Januk's Berkeley V Adolfe, CD, CS, CGC, TT (aka Mac, a Rottweiler)

Contents

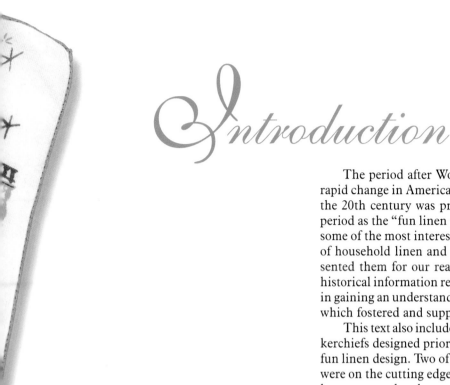

Introduction

The period after World War II and through the 1960s was a time of rapid change in American society. Since a large portion of the fun linen of the 20th century was produced within this time frame, we refer to this period as the "fun linen period" throughout this text. We have assembled some of the most interesting as well as some of the more typical examples of household linen and handkerchief designs from this period and presented them for our readers. They are organized by subject matter and historical information relating to each subject is provided to aid the reader in gaining an understanding of the political and social climate in America, which fostered and supported this humorous and unique design period.

This text also includes signed and unsigned household linen and handkerchiefs designed prior to the "fun linen period" by early proponents of fun linen design. Two of these early designers, Tony Sarg and Tom Lamb, were on the cutting edge in terms of designing fun textiles. Many of their humorous and anthropomorphic textile designs were made prior to World War II, during a time when more traditional and realistic designs were the norm. Their contributions to 20th century fun household linen and handkerchief design are difficult to ignore.

After World War II, America was rapidly changing and gravitating toward unprecedented prosperity. The baby boom, suburban living, automobiles, air conditioning, improved highways, television, and eventually air travel all contributed to a rapidly changing American way of life, and thereby influenced the design of fun household linen and handkerchiefs. For example, higher disposable incomes, better highways, increased automobile ownership, air conditioning, and air travel encouraged the growth of tourism. This led to increased demand for souvenirs, which fostered the design of maps and city scenes on fun linen. Several examples of maps printed on tablecloths, handkerchiefs, and an apron are included in Chapter 9, Geography and Travel. Suburban living also had a tremendous influence on fun linen design. Along with suburban living came backyard barbecues, a marked increase in home entertaining, hide-a-bars, and theme parties. All of these contributed to the design of wonderful fun textiles, particularly those represented in Chapters 5 and 8, which focus on cocktails and food.

Changes in gender roles in America, which occurred simultaneously with the factors mentioned earlier, also significantly influenced the design of household linen and handkerchiefs. World War II was a catalyst for these changing roles. During the War, women formed a vital part of the American workforce by filling the void in factories and other workplaces that had resulted from so many men being sent to the European and Pacific Theaters. They also served in various branches of the armed forces. At the same time, many American men and women in the armed forces were experiencing new cultures as they served in other countries, and they too were undergoing significant changes in their lives. Not surprisingly, both sexes' perceptions of themselves changed as a result of

Opposite page: *Description:* Television Handkerchief, Pat Prichard
Pat Prichard designed the linen handkerchief pictured on the adjoining page. Some of our readers may remember this type of television design from the 1950s. The pictures were often blurry, reception could be spotty, and irritating static often occurred at the most inopportune times. This was certainly a far cry from digital television! The colors in this handkerchief have faded slightly and the fabric is starting to show wear. Pat Prichard also designed a second television theme handkerchief, an example of which is pictured on p. 86 of Roseanna Mihalick's book, *Collecting Handkerchiefs.*
Measurements: 14.625"L x 14.75"W
Price Range:
$20-22
$10-12 poor condition

their wartime roles. After the War, both men and women returned to peacetime America faced with the task of reconciling these changed perceptions with their traditional roles in society. As you will see, a significant amount of the household linen and handkerchiefs produced during this time reflects these changes. The items portray a society where men and women were assuming new roles, the women's liberation movement was gaining momentum, and discussions about love and sex were no longer in poor taste or held only behind closed doors. One has only to think of Woodstock in 1969 to realize the extent to which American society changed during this period. The household linen and handkerchiefs are documentaries unto themselves.

The majority of the household linen and handkerchiefs presented in this text were made exclusively for the American market. However, there are also a few examples of pieces purchased in Europe by American tourists, either for use in their homes or as souvenirs from their travel. As used in this text, the term "household linen" refers to textiles made specifically for use in the home. We have included examples of aprons, bedspreads, curtains, cushion covers, doilies, laundry bags, napkins, napkin rings, pillowcases, placemats, potholders, runners, tablecloths, and towels. "Table linen" refers to a specific group of household linen made for use while dining, such as tablecloths, napkins, placemats, napkin rings, and runners. Household linen in the 20th century was made with a variety of natural and synthetic textiles, such as linen, cotton, and polyester, to name a few. It was also not uncommon for pieces to be made with a mixture of these natural and synthetic fibers.

Printed household linen and handkerchiefs constitute the majority of items illustrated in this text. Since this is the case, we do not make a note of it in the captions when an item is printed. Printed household linen and handkerchiefs were very popular throughout the 20th century because they were easy to maintain and readily available at reasonable prices, especially when compared to hand-made items. Production of hand-made household linen continued to decline as the century progressed for a number of reasons. As more women began to work outside the home, their changing lifestyles resulted in less leisure time to devote to embroidery, crochet, and other home craft projects. At the same time, with increased prosperity came higher wages, which meant labor-intensive products such as hand-embroidered household linen became increasingly expensive. Faced with less time to make their own household linen coupled with escalating prices for hand-made items available in the stores, many women found printed household linen to be an attractive alternative.

Although the popularity of hand-made household linen continued to decline during the second half of the 20th century, its contribution to fun linen design in the 20th century cannot be ignored. A considerable amount of fun linen, especially cocktail napkins and towels, was embroidered. Therefore, this text also includes many examples of embroidered items, including cross-stitch, cutwork, and appliqué. Crochet and hand-painted household linen are also included. It should be noted that hand-painted household linen was not very popular in the 20th century. This was possibly due to the problem of the paint flaking off so quickly when the linen was laundered. Consequently, very few examples are available today.

Many of the examples in this text are signed and copyrighted, and they are noted as such in the captions. Most signed household linen and handkerchiefs can be dated to the postwar period. Chapter 16 provides information about some of the popular American textile designers we have featured. However, even though we have included numerous examples of signed handkerchiefs, aprons, towels, napkins, placemats and tablecloths, our readers should not assume that the majority of 20th century household linen and handkerchiefs was signed. As noted in Chapter 16, textile designers have traditionally been an anonymous group in America and little is actually known about most of them. Consequently, the vast majority of collectible 20th century textiles are unsigned and almost impossible to attribute to specific designers or manufacturers. This statement remains true as we enter the 21st century.

Many of the items shown in this text are politically incorrect by late 20th century and current standards. However, at the time they were produced the majority of the American public found them to be amusing. They were used in American homes on a daily basis and for the purpose of entertaining. As authors we are simply presenting history. We hope our readers will not be offended in any way by the subject matter contained in this text and the chapters devoted to naughty ladies and cocktails and spirits in particular.

Our selection criteria for items to include were simple: **The items are collectible, cheerful, and fun**. We selected them in the hope that they would bring smiles to the faces of our readers, young and old, and fond memories to those old enough to remember the days when these items experienced their "heyday." In addition, we selected many of them as documentaries of a changing America.

Readers often ask us where to purchase collectible household linen and handkerchiefs. Many of the examples shown here can be purchased at estate sales, flea markets, antique shops, auctions, and antique shows. Admittedly, some of the examples are difficult to obtain and when this is the case we have noted their scarcity in the caption. Of course, availability is often dependent on geographic location. Crocheted items, for instance, are more readily available in country venues than in city shops.

With a few exceptions, the examples presented in this text are from the authors' collections. We have noted the source for examples that are not owned by either of us. Almost all of the pieces in the text are in mint, excellent, very good, or good condition as defined below:

Mint condition: These items have never been used and still retain their original paper labels. They may also come in their original boxes or folders, which should also be in undamaged condition. The items must not be faded, damaged, or stained. Items that have stains along their fold lines from improper storage cannot be considered as mint. Many of these fold line stains cannot be removed by washing the article. The buyer should beware when someone says that all such stains will come out in the wash.

Excellent condition: These items meet all the criteria for mint condition except they do not have their original paper labels. They may or may not have their original boxes or folders. The condition of the box or folder is not important. Marks such as faint glue residue where a paper label was once attached or fold line stains, regardless of how faint, would eliminate these items from the excellent condition category.

Very Good condition: These items are not faded and do not have any stains (with one exception, noted below), holes, tears, frayed edges, or missing parts. In terms of stains, the only exception would be faint marks where a paper label was attached. The items may have been washed a few times; however, the fabric should still be very sturdy. Items that have been washed to the point where the fabric feels very limp and appears thin do not belong in this category.

Good condition: These items meet all the criteria for very good condition except for some minor stains, which we consider minimal damage.

Household linen or handkerchiefs that do not meet the above criteria are not considered collectible unless they are extremely rare. When an item does not fall into one of the four condition categories listed above, we have noted this in the caption. Where applicable, we also have noted the difference in price between items that fall into one of the above condition categories versus those that do not. Having said this, the reader should not assume damaged items are totally worthless. Such items may still be used for the purposes they were originally intended or cut up and incorporated into quilts, cushion covers, and other interesting textile products. It is important to note, however, that *useful* is not synonymous with *collectible*. For the purposes of this text, collectible items are defined as pieces that we believe have the potential to appreciate in value in the future.

Labels are found on many of the items we have featured and some of the items are in their original folders. When items are in excellent condition the label or original packaging enhances their value and makes it likely that they will command a premium price when purchased or sold. Nonetheless, the condition of the item is the most important consideration when purchasing or selling it. Therefore, when given the choice between an item in *good* condition *with* the original labels and the same item in *excellent* condition *without* original labels, we recommend purchasing the latter. This recommendation also holds true for original packaging.

A variety of furniture styles have been used to display the linen we have assembled for this text. This was purposefully done to emphasize the possibilities for using collectible 20th century household linen in the home. The internationally acclaimed furniture designer and woodworker, George Nakashima (1905-1990), designed the modern walnut and cherry furniture shown on pages 10, 22, 32, 49, 52, 82, 93, 111, 136, and 145. Mr. Nakashima was at the forefront of the American Craft Revival after World War II. His work was innovative and incorporated the natural forms of trees.

In conclusion, this text takes the reader on a journey through a rapidly changing America as seen through the household linen and handkerchiefs designed by some of the most famous as well as many anonymous textile designers who worked primarily in the "fun linen period." We hope our readers will find countless hours of enjoyment on this journey.

1.1 Description: It's a Cat's Life Cocktail Napkins Folder
The folder by Leacock & Company, Inc. contains eight hand-printed linen napkins with Siamese cats
assuming human poses. The cats seem to be living the good life. They are pictured dancing, shaving,
drinking, and relaxing. They are not your average cats in very much the same way Yogi was not your
average bear. The folder has plastic binding, a see-through cover, and four plastic pages. The plastic
pages hold eight napkins and the first napkin in the folder serves as the cover. This is our first
example of animals portraying human behavior. Hold on to your seats! There are many more to follow.
Measurements: 8.75"L x 6.25"W
Price Range: $35-45

Animals were a favorite subject matter for household linen and handkerchief designers throughout the 20th century. As we searched our collections and the marketplace, we found hundreds of examples of fun household linen and handkerchiefs with animal motifs. We could have easily filled an entire book using animals as the theme.

Early in the 20th century, animals were generally represented on household linen and adult handkerchiefs as we usually see them in reality: sitting, standing, running, and playing in natural poses. As the century progressed, anthropomorphism gradually crept into textile designs. This trend reached its peak during the "fun linen period," when animals exhibiting human behavior were a popular and recurring theme for designers of household linen and handkerchiefs. Although old familiar poses were still used frequently, many animals featured on textiles during this period bear only a passing resemblance to animals in real life. The animals portrayed on many of the items shown in this text make the viewer feel very much like Alice must have felt when she encountered the Cheshire cat! One can only marvel at the incredible imaginations of the textile designers who created these pieces.

Many collectors prefer to collect a particular animal or breed of animal. For example, they may favor dogs, cats, horses, or elephants. Dogs were the most collectible animals found on 20th century household linen and adult handkerchiefs. They were most often seen on towels and cocktail napkins and rarely seen on other household linen. Poodles were the breed most readily portrayed. Poodles are represented in almost every chapter in this text. They are doing all sorts of things including traveling to Paris to shop at the canine equivalent of Dior (which is referred to as Dore on the towel pictured as Item 9.18).

Cats were the second most popular species of animals found on household linen and adult handkerchiefs during the 20th century. In a similar fashion to dogs, they were most often seen on towels and cocktail napkins and rarely seen on other household linen. Siamese cats were the most popular breed. The Siamese cat napkins (Item 1.1) and towels (Item 1.2) seen in this chapter are very collectible.

Horses were another popular subject matter for household linen and adult handkerchief designers. Although representations of horses tended to be traditional throughout the century, they were occasionally presented in non-traditional poses and colors. Item 1.28 in this chapter depicts a talking horse. The movie *Francis The Talking Mule* opened in movie theaters in 1949 and *Mr. Ed*, the talking horse television series, was a big hit in the 1960s. Therefore, it is not surprising that textiles depicting talking animals were popular in the 20th century.

Animals portraying human behavior appeared on children's handkerchiefs early in the 20th century and such anthropomorphic designs on children's handkerchiefs continued to be produced throughout the "fun linen period." Tom Lamb and Disney designed many of the pre-World War II signed children's handkerchiefs. It is relatively easy to amass a collection of children's handkerchiefs by Disney or Tom Lamb. There are still a large number of wonderful designs to be found at reasonable prices in today's marketplace. There are also excellent examples of unsigned children's handkerchiefs.

Some of the most famous animals to appear in 20th century children's handkerchiefs are well-known Disney characters such as Mickey and Minnie Mouse and Pluto. Mickey Mouse children's handkerchiefs from the 1930s, which resemble the one shown as Item 1.32, are scarce and very collectible. Later Mickey handkerchiefs are also popular. They are easier to locate and considerably less expensive than the 1930s examples.

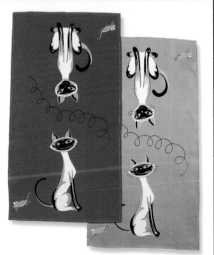

1.2 Description: Siamese Cat Towels
Each towel has a cat on one end smiling with a mouse to its left and a cat on the other end licking its lips. Since there is also a mouse to the left of the cat licking its lips, we are not sure if the cat is licking its lips because it has already eaten a mouse or because it is anticipating eating the mouse to its left. You be the judge. An orange colored version of this towel was featured in the July 2001 issue of Martha Stewart's magazine, *Living.*
Measurements: 28.5"L x 15.5"W
Price Range: $20-30 either color

1.3 Description: Dog Handkerchiefs and Towels, Tammis Keefe
The towels and handkerchiefs shown are very well known, highly collectible designs by Tammis Keefe. In addition to the colors featured here, we have seen the towel with aqua and pink backgrounds and the handkerchief in gray, brown, and yellow. It is likely there are additional color combinations. The blue and red versions shown here are the most common and desirable colors. Dogs were a favorite subject matter for Tammis Keefe and she produced at least four additional handkerchief designs with dogs. She also designed scarves. We have seen four silk scarf designs with dogs as the subject matter. Even though the design pictured here is the most common of her canine designs, it is also the most popular. We often see both the towels and the handkerchiefs with their original paper labels. The paper labels on the towels say Belgian linen and the handkerchiefs have the distinctive J. H. Kimball & Company, Inc. yellow and gold label. Some of the towels have Fallani & Cohn labels sewn into their hems.
Measurements:
14.5" square, handkerchief
29"L x 16"W, towel
Price Range:
$30-35 red or blue handkerchief
$20-25 handkerchief, other colors
$35-45 towel

1.4 Description: Cat Handkerchiefs and Towels, Tammis Keefe
Another collection of loved and well-known designs by Tammis Keefe is shown in both the handkerchief and towel versions. We have seen the cat towels in blue, aqua, and red, which are the same color versions we have seen for the dog towels. In addition to the gray version shown, the handkerchiefs were also made in the same blue and red as the dogs as well as several other colors. The blue cat towel is in poor condition. It has been washed numerous times and the color is noticeably faded especially when compared to the blue on the dog towel. The gray handkerchief has also been washed numerous times and Tammis Keefe's signature has partially disappeared. The blue cat handkerchief is in mint condition with the original J. H. Kimball & Company, Inc. yellow and gold label in one corner. Like the dogs, the blue and red versions of the handkerchief are the most popular versions. Tammis Keefe created at least three other handkerchief designs and at least one other towel design with cat motifs.
Measurements:
14.5" square, handkerchief
29"L x 16"W, towel
Price Range:
$20-25 red or blue handkerchief
$18-22 handkerchief, other colors
$10-12 gray handkerchief, poor condition
$28-30 towel
$10-12 blue towel, poor condition

1.5 Description: Intoxicated Animals Cocktail Napkins
Six napkins from a set of twelve are shown. The linen napkins feature whimsical intoxicated animals drinking from bottles. The designer of this set of napkins cleverly produced the various animals in both positive and negative color versions to create an interesting variation.
Measurements: 7.5"L x 5.5"W
Price Range: $28-36 set of twelve

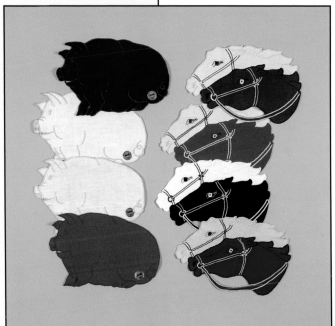

1.6 Description: Figural Horse and Pig Cocktail Napkins
The paper labels on these napkins read "An Exclusive Creation, Imperial, Hand Embroidered in Madeira, Portugal, Pure Linen." The quality of the embroidery on both sets is excellent. The pig napkins were made in four colors. The set came with two napkins in each color in their original Saks Fifth Avenue box. The horse head napkins have two horse heads in different color combinations on each napkin. There are four different color combinations and there are two napkins with each color combination in the set. Very few cocktail napkins with figural shapes were produced during the "fun linen period." Both sets of napkins are very collectible and difficult to find.
Measurements:
5"L x 7.625"W, horse napkins
5"L x 7.875"W, pig napkins
Price Range: $135-150 each set of eight

1.7 Description: Poodle Handkerchiefs, Jean Hannau
The poodle on the gold handkerchief is dressed in her afternoon finery. She is being admired and pursued by several gentlemen while visiting Place Pigalle. Note the bird in the tree observing the scene. The poodle on the blue handkerchief is enjoying the cancan being performed by other poodles. Both handkerchiefs are signed Jean Hannau.
Measurements: 15"L x 15.5"W
Price Range: $40-50 each handkerchief

1.8 Description: Playful Cats Handkerchief, Liliane; and Mischievous Cat Cocktail Napkins, Tammis Keefe
Whimsical cats are playing on the handkerchief on the top of this photo. The handkerchief is signed Liliane and has the original tag that reads "*Bloch Frères* linen." Another Liliane handkerchief, not pictured here, utilizes the same color scheme and features cats chasing birds. Four napkins from a set of eight signed by Tammis Keefe are shown below the handkerchief. There is a different scene on each napkin shown. The set has two napkins with each design. The napkins tell the story of a bird escaping from its cage and a mischievous cat. The first napkin has an open birdcage with a sign that says "out to lunch"; the second napkin shows the bird out of the cage; the third napkin has only feathers; and the last napkin shows a contented cat. We leave the conclusion of this story to your imagination. Sylvester, the cat, eat your heart out! This set of napkins originally came in a gold colored gift box with a clear cellophane center on the cover. Printed on the lower right corner of the top are the words "Pure Linen Cocktail Napkins, Set of Eight, A Falflax Original." The napkins were also made with figures in olive green on the same cream background pictured here.
Measurements:
14" square, handkerchief
8.25" square, napkins
Price Range:
$25-35 handkerchief
$35-45 set of eight napkins

13

1.10 Description: Close-up of Item 1.9

1.9 Description: Crocheted Scottish Terrier Runner
The figural crocheted runner in this Christmas scene has three cute Scottish Terriers pictured on it. Figural crochet with animals as subject matter is difficult to find. This runner would make a lovely addition to a crochet collection.
Measurements: 29"L x 12"W
Price Range: $20-30

1.11 Description: Puppies and Kittens Tablecloth
Red puppies and kittens are romping all over this tablecloth. It is a charming design that never fails to bring a smile to one's face. Printed tablecloths with dogs or cats as subject matter are scarce. Embroidered dog or cat tablecloths are more common.
This particular design was also printed on a lighter weight material with a pink, burgundy, and apple green color scheme.
This tablecloth was hand printed by Broderie Creations and made in the United States. It retailed for less than $1.50 when it was originally produced.
Measurements: 50.5"L x 45"W
Price Range: $55-65

1.12 *Description:* Cat Kitchen Towel
This cheerful kitchen towel shows a cat serving cheese *à la mouse* on a tray. There are photographs of the cat's ancestors in the picture frames on the upper right and left-hand sides of the towel. The photographs give the impression this is a very upper-class household. After all, not every household has a cat that serves mice meals on a tray. Whatever happened to cheese and crackers? The label on the towel reads "Fallani and Cohn, Pure Linen."
Measurements: 30"L x 16.5"W
Price Range: $15-18

1.13 *Description:* Girl with Horse Towels
This towel is shown in two different colors. The towels depict a simple yet effective scene of a girl and her horse silhouetted in a doorway. The red towel has a small tear along the upper left-hand edge.
Measurements: 19.75"L x 13.75"W
Price Range:
$15-18 either color
$6-8 poor condition

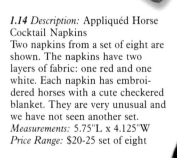

1.14 *Description:* Appliquéd Horse Cocktail Napkins
Two napkins from a set of eight are shown. The napkins have two layers of fabric: one red and one white. Each napkin has embroidered horses with a cute checkered blanket. They are very unusual and we have not seen another set.
Measurements: 5.75"L x 4.125"W
Price Range: $20-25 set of eight

1.15 *Description:* Ladies Riding Horses Handkerchief
Ladies in period costume riding sidesaddle are silhouetted throughout this handkerchief. It is signed *Deposé* in one corner and the fabric label sewn into one edge reads "a Skandia print, copyright 1963, Robinson & Golluber, Inc."
Measurements: 12"L x 12.375"W
Price Range: $8-12

1.16 *Description:* Printed Horses Tablecloth
The equine design on this tablecloth is unusual. Most tablecloths with horses depict hunting or racing scenes. The sense of movement in this scene is fabulous. The fabric label sewn on one edge of the tablecloth reads "Simtex, Made Right In America."
Measurements: 68"L x 54.25"W
Price Range: $65-75

1.17 *Description:* Appliquéd Organdy Horse Centerpiece
The hand-embroidered appliquéd linen horse on this very fine organdy centerpiece has tiny French knots to define facial features and musculature and create shadows for a more three-dimensional effect than the norm in appliqué. Most appliqué embroidery simply attaches an extra piece of material on top of another fabric either by hand or machine stitching. Very simple raised stitches were also added to create further definition. Additional embellishment with hand embroidery similar to the work in this piece was done only for the high-end market since the additional material and labor costs made this level of detail expensive to produce. This piece was made in Madeira in the 1970s.
Measurements: 12.5"L x 22.5"W
Price Range: $55-60

1.18 *Description:* Jungle Print Handkerchief and Towels, Tammis Keefe
The towels and the handkerchief shown here are very collectible pieces signed by Tammis Keefe. The tiger towel is the most difficult piece of the three to find. Both towels retain their original Belgian linen paper labels. The subject matter on the handkerchief is puzzling. Why are there three smiling leopard faces and one face with a pout?
Measurements:
30"L x 16.5"W, each towel
14.5" square, handkerchief
Price Range:
$35-45 each towel
$30-40 handkerchief

1.19 Description: Zebra Handkerchief, Mary Blair
A linen handkerchief by Mary Blair depicting stylized zebras in fantastic colors is shown here. Its original paper label reads "Studio of Carol Stanley, White Linen, Hand Rolled." Handkerchiefs by Mary Blair are difficult to find and highly collectible.
Measurements: 13"L x 13.5"W
Price Range: $65-80

1.20 Description: Saggy Baggy Elephant Handkerchief and Little Golden Book
This children's handkerchief was produced as an advertising tie-in for the 1947 edition of the Little Golden Book titled *The Saggy Baggy Elephant*, also pictured here. Gustaf Tenggren created the design for the handkerchief shown and illustrated the book.
Measurements: 9.25"L x 9.5"W
Price Range: $15-20

1.21 Description: Elephants and Lions Handkerchief, Peg Thomas
Tammis Keefe also signed the name Peg Thomas on her designs. This example is one of the easiest Tammis Keefe designs to find with the Peg Thomas signature. The original J. H. Kimball & Company, Inc. paper label is attached. This humorous design is always popular with handkerchief collectors. Tammis Keefe used motifs inspired by India on one other handkerchief signed by Peg Thomas. The second handkerchief features only people. A photograph of the second handkerchief appears in an article about Tammis Keefe in the April/May 2000 issue of *American Craft* magazine.
Measurements: 14.5" square
Price Range: $30-35

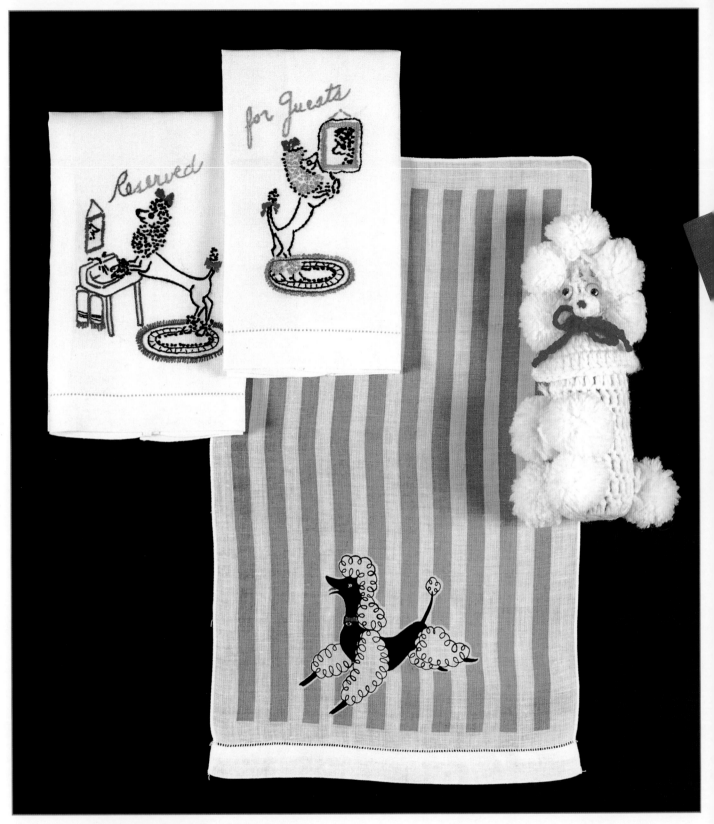

1.22 Description: Poodles Made To Make You Smile

The large striped towel features a poodle with a beaded eye and a rhinestone on its collar. This towel is not difficult to find and is a popular collectible. The pair of embroidered poodle guest towels at the top left-hand corner will bring a smile to the face of every guest who uses the powder room. The poodles on the towels are in the bathroom. One poodle is washing its paws and looking in the mirror and the other poodle is just looking in the mirror. The words "reserved for guests" are embroidered on the towels. The cute crocheted bottle cover that accompanies the towels in this picture was a popular item in American homes in the 1950s. This type of item was mainly used for decoration.

Measurements:
18"L x 11"W, striped towel
19"L x 12.5"W, embroidered towels
9" high, crocheted bottle cover

Price Range:
$22-25 striped towel
$28-35 embroidered towel set
$10-15 crocheted bottle cover

1.23 *Description:* Appliquéd Scottish Terriers Tablecloth and Napkins

This Scottish Terriers tablecloth and four matching napkins were designed for a child's table. The design may be unique since we have not seen another example. Household linen made specifically for children's furniture is difficult to find.
Measurements:
24" square, tablecloth
10" square, napkins
Price Range: $25-35 five-piece set

1.24 *Description:* Terrier Lipstick Towel
The West Highland White Terrier embroidered on this hand towel is looking in the mirror. Lipstick towels are very collectible. They were made in red to prevent lipstick smears from being too obvious if the towels were used to blot ladies' lipstick.
Measurements: 14.5"L x 8.5"W
Price Range: $18-22

1.25 *Description:* Poodle Apron
This is a very eye-catching apron from the 1950s with poodles and red and white polka dots.
Measurements: 19"L x 21.5"W, gathered at the waist
Price Range: $20-25

19

1.26 *Description:* Pony Tablecloth
This 1940s tablecloth showing a cute little pony is a very nice tablecloth for a child's birthday party. It would also make an interesting wall hanging for a child's room.
Measurements: 52"L x 48"W
Price range: $25-40

1.27 *Description:* Democratic Party Handkerchief, Jeanne Miller
Vote Democratic! This linen handkerchief is signed Jeanne Miller and features donkeys, the traditional mascots of the Democratic Party, in non-traditional shades of pink. Among the 20th century handkerchief designers, Jeanne Miller, Pat Prichard, and Don are known to have made signed handkerchiefs with the Democratic and Republican parties as the subject matter.
Measurements: 14.25" square
Price Range: $20-22

1.28 *Description:* Happy Birthday Handkerchief, Welcher
Welcher designed this linen happy birthday handkerchief featuring several smiling talking horses in very striking colors. This handkerchief would be a fun birthday gift for someone who loves horses.
Measurements: 14.25" square
Price Range: $18-20

1.29 *Description:* Dog Cocktail Napkin Sets, Vera
These linen napkin sets are atypical Vera designs since she was best known for floral designs. There are eight napkins in each set. Both sets have Vera's signature without the ladybug on the lower right-hand corners. The yellow napkins came in their original cardboard box and have their original round paper labels stating they were made with Irish linen. Unfortunately, they have apparently been stored for a long time pinned together with steel staples, which left tiny rust spots where they touched the fabric. The rust marks should disappear when the napkins are washed. The Dalmatian on the fire engine is a great example of an animal in a very traditional setting rendered very untraditional by its fantastic, fantasy color. Whoever heard of a red Dalmatian?
Measurements:
7.25"L x 5.25"W, yellow napkins
5.25"L x 7.25"W, fire engine napkins
Price Range:
$40-45 each set of eight napkins
$34-36 yellow set in good condition pictured

1.30 *Description:* Dog Kitchen Towel
This towel features a Poodle, Husky, Terrier, Dachshund, and Doberman in traditional poses. Bones form an interesting border for the towel.
Measurements: 26"L x 15" W
Price Range: $25-35

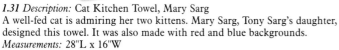

1.31 *Description:* Cat Kitchen Towel, Mary Sarg
A well-fed cat is admiring her two kittens. Mary Sarg, Tony Sarg's daughter, designed this towel. It was also made with red and blue backgrounds.
Measurements: 28"L x 16"W
Price Range: $18-20

1.32 *Description:* Mickey Mouse and Donald Duck Handkerchief
This 1930s children's handkerchief features Mickey Mouse and Donald Duck. Note how thin Donald is on this handkerchief compared to the portrayal of him on the mid-20th century handkerchief (Item 14.11). This handkerchief was also made with a red background.
Measurements: 8"L x 8.75"W
Price Range: $40-45

2.1 Description: Chenille Bedspread
The chenille bedspread pictured above has a double peacock design. There are twelve hearts on the bedspread with three flowers inside each heart. This bedspread is very collectible because of the double peacock scene and the hearts.
Measurements: 100"L x 92"W
Price Range: $125-175

Chapter 2
Birds

Birds fascinate people the world over. Large numbers of Americans belong to associations that watch and protect birds. It is likely that our fascination with these charming creatures is a result of our curiosity about their ability to fly, their spectacular colors, the array of species, and the melodies many of them provide that uplift our hearts. Therefore, it is not surprising that birds were a popular topic for household linen and handkerchief designs throughout the 20th century.

Prior to World War II, representations of birds on household linen were generally traditional. Wild birds were more common subject matter than domestic birds such as ducks and chickens. This was possibly due to the popularity of hunting themes, which incorporated wild ducks, geese, or pheasants. After World War II and into the 1960s, during the height of popularity of 20th century fun linen, birds were increasingly depicted in non-traditional poses.

Roosters were the most common birds represented on household linen during the 20th century. This appears to coincide with the growth in popularity of cocktail napkins. Although the actual origin of the cocktail is unknown, the following anecdote may indicate the source of the strong association between roosters and cocktails.

As legend has it, in 1779 American soldiers with gin and French soldiers with vermouth blended these beverages together and stirred them with tail feathers taken from Mrs. Betsy Flanagan's roosters at Flanagan's Inn of Tarrytown and White Plains. Another version of this tale places the same enterprising soldiers at Peggy Van Eyck's Cock's Tail Tavern in Yonkers, New York.

Regardless of the veracity of this story, the fact remains that there are an astonishing variety of wild rooster designs on cocktail napkins from the 20th century. Interesting examples of rooster motifs on cocktail napkins are shown as Items 2.15 and 2.18.

Peacocks were also popular subject matter on household linen during the "fun linen period." Chenille bedspreads with peacock motifs from the 1950s and 1960s are particularly memorable and truly capture the spirit of fun household linen. It seems the rule of thumb when designing a peacock bedspread in those decades was the more elaborate and colorful, the better. The most collectible peacock chenilles are some of the most eye-catching examples of household linen from the 20th century. This chapter begins with a wonderful example of a double peacock chenille bedspread (Item 2.1) on the adjoining page. This type of bedspread design is currently very popular with collectors.

Items with roosters and peacocks currently appear to be the most collectible subject matter for collectors of 20th century bird motif household linen and they usually command the highest prices. The popularity of roosters and peacocks may be due in part to the astonishing number of colors that can be incorporated into their tails.

Adult handkerchiefs with bird motifs are not particularly collectible at this time. The popularity of peacocks and roosters on household linen in the "fun linen period" did not extend to handkerchief designs. Peacocks very rarely appear on handkerchiefs. Roosters appear occasionally but not with any noteworthy regularity. In a fashion similar to household linen, birds are often pictured in non-traditional poses on handkerchiefs made after World War II.

Disney's Donald Duck was the most popular bird on 20th century children's handkerchiefs. He appears in countless human poses from the 1930s until the end of the handkerchief era. He was the duck of the century! Other famous cartoon birds that appeared on children's handkerchiefs include Chilly Willy, Tweety Bird, Woody Woodpecker, and Heckle and Jeckle. Examples of children's handkerchiefs depicting any of these characters are difficult to find.

In keeping with the recurring anthropomorphic theme in 20th century fun household linen and handkerchiefs, many of the birds in this chapter are seen in non-traditional colors and assuming human behavior. Roosters and other birds are pictured sitting in martini glasses, sleeping in brandy glasses, drinking, smoking, and generally being merry.

2.2 Description: Farmers and Chickens Kitchen Towel
"Chicken today, Feathers tomorrow!" The farmer and his wife shown on this towel seem to be positively thrilled at this thought. Bright green and pink chickens add to the "zany" quality of this kitchen towel. This towel was also made in a red and darker green color combination and a brown and yellow version. There is a companion towel that shows a chicken actually in the driver's seat, apparently driving the farmer's truck. The scenes on both of these towels were also used on a tablecloth. An example of the tablecloth can be seen in the book entitled *More Terrific Tablecloths*, by Loretta Smith Fehling.
Measurements: 27"L x 15.625"W
Price Range:
$10-12 pink and green version
$15-17 red and dark green version (not pictured)
$6-8 yellow and brown version (not pictured)

2.4 *Description:*
Crocheted Bird
Potholder
This type of potholder
was often made for
church bazaars and
craft shows in the mid-
20th century. It is
shown with a teapot
designed by Michael
Graves for Alessi. The
teapot dates from the
fourth quarter of the
20th century.
Measurements: 5.5"L x
4.75"W
Price Range: $8-10

2.3 *Description:* Chickens Card Tablecloth
This linen tablecloth has hens and roosters on each corner. The scene
on each corner is different and only half of the tablecloth is pictured
here. The unusual aspects of this tablecloth are the feathers on each
chicken, which are actually different suits of playing cards. The
chickens shown here have diamonds, spades, and clubs. The border
consists of different colored eggs. This is a fun tablecloth for entertaining guests for bridge or other card games. This design was also used on
a 72" long tablecloth in a red, brown, and black color combination.
Tammis Keefe designed the poodle playing cards shown here.
Measurements: 51" square
Price Range: $45-50

2.5 *Description:* Singing Birds Handkerchiefs, Virginia Zito
Virginia Zito designed this linen handkerchief with singing birds in two colors. Although
many birds sing, like Alice, we know we must have fallen down the rabbit hole when the
birds wear necklaces and sunglasses! A companion handkerchief (not pictured) depicts
similar birds interspersed with flower beds.
Measurements: 15.125"L x 14.875"W
Price Range: $17-19 each color

2.6 Description: Stylized Roosters Tablecloth
This Eames era tablecloth is collectible because of the stylized designs. Only one quarter of the tablecloth is shown. There is a large rooster on each corner and various stylized fish, roosters, and pitchers are scattered on the tablecloth.
Measurements: 50" square
Price Range: $25-45

2.7 Description: Children's Round Duck Handkerchief
This adorable duck is wearing a charming beret with matching shoes and a bow tie. The handkerchief is an appealing collectible for those who collect round handkerchiefs and/or children's handkerchiefs. Unfortunately, the machine-embroidered edge has started to separate from the fabric in one area. We consider this example to be in poor condition.
Measurements: 9" diameter
Price Range:
$18-20
$4-5 poor condition

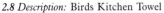

2.8 Description: Birds Kitchen Towel
This striped towel with hand embroidery was made for the kitchen. It features a blue bird sleeping in a brandy glass with a second blue bird on the rim of the glass singing. We hope the blue bird on the bottom of the glass has not been drinking too much brandy.
Measurements: 27.5"L x 15"W
Price Range: $10-12

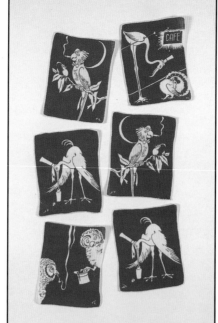

2.10 Description: Drunken Bird Cocktail Napkins
The birds on this set of six red and white napkins are displaying surprising behavior. We never imagined a stork drinking alcohol or a parrot and an owl smoking. It is likely this is a set of eight with two napkins missing.
Measurements: 7.75"L x 5.25"W
Price Range: $25-35 set of six

2.9 Description: Bird and Urn Kitchen Towel
This hand-embroidered striped kitchen towel features a red bird looking at its reflections in an urn. The bird seems happy with what it sees.
Measurements: 28"L x 15"W
Price Range: $10-12

2.11 Description: Peacock Cushion Cover
A beautiful peacock is walking among the flowers on this hand-embroidered linen cushion cover. The crocheted border of the cover is also hand made. It provides an effective finishing touch.
Measurements: 15"L x 23.25"W
Price Range: $25-28

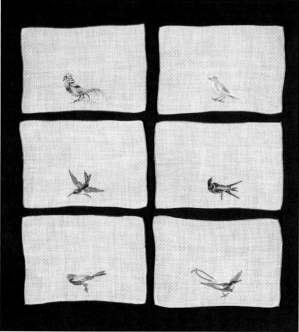

2.12 Description: Cocktail Napkins with Petit Point Birds
The napkins in this set are fun and elegant. The quality of the petit point is very good. There are twelve napkins in the set.
Measurements: 5"L x 7.75"W
Price Range: $45-60 set of twelve

2.13 Description: Pheasants Tablecloth, Virginia Zito
Virginia Zito designed this tablecloth with printed pheasants, flowers, and leaves going around the edge. She is best known for her handkerchiefs and few collectors know that she also designed tablecloths, towels, and cocktail napkins. Consequently, tablecloths similar to the one pictured here and in Chapter 3, Item 3.9, are readily found at very reasonable prices in today's marketplace. Actually, her signed tablecloths typically sell in the same price range as comparable quality unsigned tablecloths. This design is more traditional than most of her other designs. The handkerchiefs pictured as Item 2.5 are more typical examples.
Measurements: 50.5" square
Price Range: $25-35

2.14 Description: Pheasants Placemat, Napkin and Runner Set
This Madeira seventeen-piece set is in mint condition. The original Leacock & Company, Inc. label is attached to the runner. The set includes a runner, eight napkins, and eight placemats. There are pheasants embroidered on each piece in the set. The napkins have a pheasant on one corner, there are two pheasants on the placemats in opposite corners, and the runner has six pairs of pheasants on its borders. The embroidery work is very good quality.
Measurements:
16.5" square, napkins
8"L x 12.2"W, placemats
14.5"L x 32.5"W, runner
Price Range: $125-140 seventeen-piece set

2.15 Description: Appliquéd Rooster Cocktail Napkins
One appliquéd napkin from a set of eight is shown. The rooster seems content sitting in the martini glass. The appliqué on this napkin is very good. Napkins with rooster motifs are perennial favorites among cocktail napkin collectors. Napkins with appliquéd roosters are more difficult to find than napkins with roosters outlined with various types of needlework stitches. Consequently, the former typically command a premium price.
Measurements: 5"L x 8"W
Price Range: $65-80 set of eight

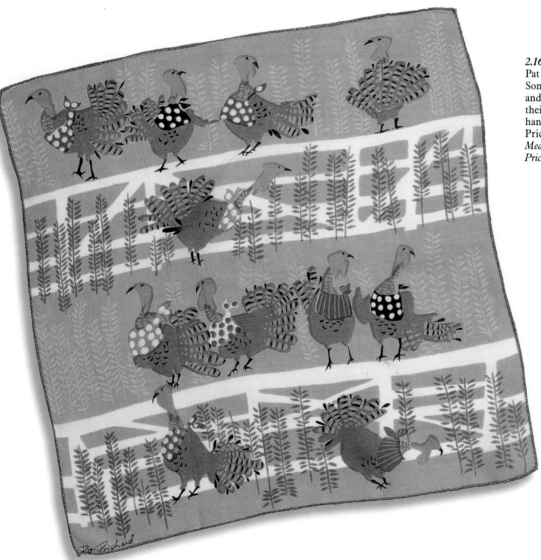

2.16 Description: Turkeys Handkerchief, Pat Prichard
Some very happy turkeys wearing red and blue-checkered kerchiefs around their necks are shown on this handkerchief designed by Pat Prichard.
Measurements: 14.5" square
Price Range: $18-20

28

2.17 Description: Embroidered Chicken and Rooster Pillowcases
The chickens on these pillowcases seem to be admiring their young.
The rooster is the more vocal of the two parents. These pillowcases
were made during the last quarter of the 20th century using old
transfer patterns.
Measurements: 30"L x 20"W
Price Range: $18-25 pair

2.18 Description: Rooster Cocktail Napkins, Fabrés
This set of eight cocktail napkins features comic roosters preparing,
serving, and drinking cocktails. Leacock & Company, Inc. produced
the set. The pattern is titled "Chanteclaire." The copyright date is
1952. Fabrés, the artist's name, is displayed in signature fashion on
each napkin.
Measurements: 8.25"L x 5.25"W
Price Range: $45-55 set of eight

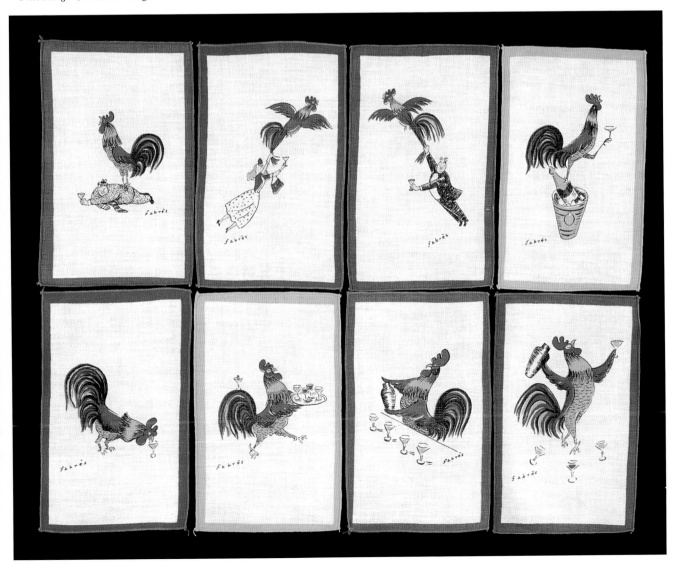

Chapter 3

Household linen and handkerchiefs were produced for many of the holidays celebrated in America. In addition to Christmas theme household linen and handkerchiefs, countless items were made to celebrate Thanksgiving, Valentine's Day, St. Patrick's Day, and Easter. Household linen was also made for birthdays and similar occasions. Handkerchiefs were made for birthdays, bon voyage presents, get well soon cards, change of address announcements, and many other important or celebratory moments. It would have been impossible to include examples for every holiday and special occasion in this chapter; therefore, we elected to restrict the chapter to one particular holiday, Christmas. We selected Christmas because household linen and handkerchiefs designed to celebrate Christmas are very popular and collectible.

The popularity of Christmas household linen and handkerchiefs in America can be easily explained. Christmas is celebrated around the world in different ways. Since there are so many people from different cultures with Christmas traditions living in America, Christmas is a very popular American holiday. Of course, not everyone celebrates Christmas. Many other religions and cultures have festivals during the month of December. For example, Kwanzaa and Hanukkah are also celebrated in December.

Although the commercialization of Christmas in America can be traced back to the 1930s, it was invigorated during the "fun linen period." Consequently, the production of Christmas household linen and handkerchiefs escalated during this period. This escalation was influenced by World War II era efforts by American citizens to send Christmas gifts to the troops abroad early. Merchants joined the effort to encourage the public to buy and send gifts early. After the War retailers promoted Christmas gift giving with even greater fervor. Vigorous promotions coupled with a booming economy resulted in increased production of Christmas theme fun linen and handkerchiefs from the mid-1940s until the 1970s.

Christmas patterns were produced on almost every form of household linen. Napkins, tablecloths, placemats, runners, towels, aprons, potholders, sheets, pillowcases, cushion covers, and bedspreads were designed to adorn the home for the Christmas season. Although most Christmas fun linen was printed, we have included two charming examples of embroidery in this chapter (Items 3.8 and 3.13).

Christmas celebrations have traditionally included some type of Christmas table linen and this practice has extended into the present. Consequently, Christmas theme linen is still considered a practical and popular gift for the holiday season. Leacock & Company, Inc. produced Christmas theme cocktail napkins in attractive gift folders. An example of a Leacock & Company, Inc. Christmas napkin set (Item 3.1) is pictured on the adjoining page. Vera also produced Christmas linen. A very interesting placemat set with holiday recipes, pictured in Chapter 8, Item 8.24, was designed by Vera. The set has a Vera Scarf Company, Inc. 1960 copyright date. Tablecloths, cocktail napkins, and towels are the most collectible Christmas household linen.

Handkerchiefs were also a popular Christmas gift for both adults and children. There are endless varieties of Christmas handkerchiefs available in the marketplace. In general, signed Christmas theme adult handkerchiefs command the highest prices and they are very collectible. In terms of children's handkerchiefs, Christmas handkerchief books are the most desirable collectibles. They are very difficult to find in good condition. The handkerchief book featured in this chapter (Item 3.7) is a wonderful example. It must have evoked a very broad smile on the face of the little child who received it for Christmas in 1941.

The examples of Christmas household linen and handkerchiefs represented in this chapter range from traditional to whimsical. The Constance Depler napkins shown on the adjoining page and the Tammis Keefe napkins and handkerchiefs (Items 3.5 and 3.11) are classic examples of anthropomorphic fun linen designs. They were designed in the mid-century period when whimsy was very popular. These four items and *The Night Before Christmas Hankies* book are the most collectible items in this chapter.

3.2 Description: Christmas Kitchen Towel, Pat Prichard The copyright on this Pat Prichard towel is dated 1955. The fabric label sewn into the hem reads "Original Town House Kitchen Decoratives, Pure Linen, Fast Color Guaranteed." This colorful linen towel has Merry Christmas in different languages written along the edges. The gold metallic paint along the border shows wear. Most printed linen towels are hardwearing and very durable; however, metallic paint similar to this usually cracks or flakes off even with very little use. Consequently, items with this type of paint are more suitable for decorative purposes. On the thinner linen used for handkerchiefs, this type of paint can actually erode the linen over time.
Measurements: 28"L x 15.5"W
Price Range:
$22-25
$12-15 poor condition

3.1 Description: Reindeer Cocktail Napkins, Constance Depler
Eight of Santa's reindeer are seen preparing for their Christmas Eve journey. The bodies of the reindeer are highlighted in gold. They are shopping, decorating the tree, and cooking. This set of napkins is representative of the whimsical Depler style. It was originally sold in a red cardboard spiral bound presentation folder with transparent plastic sleeves. The cover reads "The Cocktail Story by Leacock, Set of 8 Christmas Napkins, Hand Screen Printed Fine Irish Linen." The set pictured here does not have its folder. Ms. Depler also designed a matching towel.
Measurements: 8"L x 5.25"W
Price Range:
$30-40 set of eight napkins without folder
$45-50 set of eight napkins with the folder
$30-35 towel (not shown)

3.3 Description: Noel Towel, Tammis Keefe
This Christmas motif towel by Tammis Keefe is not difficult to find. The
linen towel was also made with a green background. The fabric label sewn
into the hem on one end reads "Fallani & Cohn, All Linen."
Measurements: 30"L x 16"W
Price Range: $18-20 either color

3.4 Description: Poinsettia Runner
Christmas theme runners are difficult to find. This example has a simple
and effective design incorporating items traditionally associated with
Christmas in the typical holiday red and green colors.
Measurements: 48"L x 15.5"W
Price Range: $25-28

3.5 Description: Drunken Reindeer Cocktail Napkins, Tammis Keefe
Santa's reindeer are obviously having a very merry time. Each of them has a drink in hand. One can only hope they are celebrating a job well done. Otherwise, Santa is in for a bumpy ride! This set of linen cocktail napkins was made in two different colors, green and red. The red version is more readily available. It is also the more popular color. These napkins were originally sold in a gold colored gift box with a clear cellophane center on the box cover.
Measurements: 7.5"L x 5.5"W
Price Range:
$65-75 set of eight napkins in red
$55-65 set of eight napkins in green

3.6 Description: Candy Cane Towels, Pat Prichard
The holly, Christmas ornaments, and candy canes on these eye-catching Pat Prichard towels evoke memories of Christmas.
Measurements: 30.75"L x 17"W
Price Range:
$20-22 green towel
$25-28 red towel

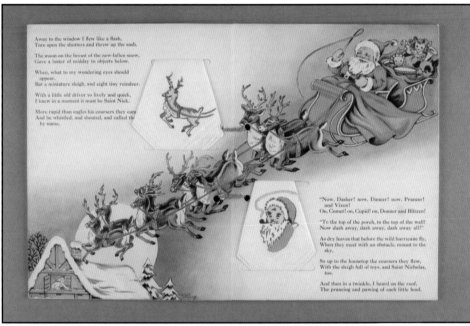

3.7 Description: The Night Before Christmas Hankies Book

This book was produced by the Herrmann Handkerchief Company in 1941. It tells the story of *The Night Before Christmas*, which was written over 150 years ago. Until recently, Clement Clarke Moore, a wealthy Manhattan biblical scholar, was believed to be the author of this tale. However, a new book titled *Author Unknown* by Don Foster, an English professor from Vassar College, presents information supporting Henry Livingston Jr., a poet of Dutch descent, as the author. According to Stephen Nissenbaum, author of *The Battle for Christmas*, the story of *The Night Before Christmas* is very important because it contributed to a new image of Santa Claus in America. Prior to the time of the poem's printing, Americans pictured St. Nicholas as a skinny, stern bishop, whereas the poem portrays him as a jovial person and contributed to turning Christmas into a time for giving. Proving the case for Henry Livingston as the author of *The Night Before Christmas* will be interesting since Moore wrote four copies of the poem by hand. One of the copies was purchased in 1997 at a Christie's auction for $211,000.

The cover of our children's handkerchief book shows Santa preparing to come down the chimney with his sack of wonderful toys. The pages of the book tell the story of *The Night Before Christmas* and contain six charming children's handkerchiefs for the holiday season. Each handkerchief has pictures around the entire border. Margot Voigt illustrated the book. The original price tag on the book's back cover reads "Schuster's Milwaukee $1.00." This book would make a wonderful Christmas gift for a children's handkerchief collector.
Measurements:
9.25"L x 7"W, book
9" square, handkerchiefs
Price Range: $325-350

3.8 *Description:* Santa Claus Cocktail Napkins
This charming set of red linen Santa cocktail napkins is machine embroidered. The color and unique shape make this set of six napkins perfect for the Christmas season. The set came in its original box.
Measurements: 7.75"L x 8.5"W
Price Range: $25-28 six napkins

3.9 *Description:* Christmas Tablecloths, Virginia Zito
The two identical linen tablecloths shown in red and green have an elegant and simple holiday design. There are gilt winged angels ringing bells centered inside the gilt harps on the corners. Giant gilt Christmas ornaments nestled in sprigs of pine decorate the borders. The tablecloths were made by Falfax and titled "Christmas Ornaments." Each tablecloth is signed by Virginia Zito. We have not seen these tablecloths in other colors.
Measurements: 52" square
Price Range: $35-55 either color

3.10 *Description:* Christmas Tablecloth, Vera
This round Christmas tablecloth by Vera is very traditional. Holly and gold horns adorn the border. The tablecloth and the six napkins are signed Vera without the ladybug. The napkins have a gold horn embellished with holly and a bow on each of them. In this photograph, the set is waiting by the fireplace to be given as a Christmas gift.
Measurements:
67" diameter, tablecloth
16.5" square, napkins
Price Range: $45-50 seven-piece set

3.11 *Description:* Santa and His Reindeer Handkerchiefs, Tammis Keefe

The two similar Tammis Keefe handkerchiefs depict merry dancing reindeer and Santas in the red and green colors traditionally associated with Christmas. These handkerchiefs were also produced with light blue and white, and pink and white backgrounds. The red and green version is much more common and more desirable. The reindeer printed on these two handkerchiefs bear a striking resemblance to the drunken reindeer on the Tammis Keefe cocktail napkins pictured as Item 3.5. This repetition of motifs with slight variations is quite typical of Tammis Keefe.

Measurements:
11.75" square, handkerchief with one Santa
14.75" square, handkerchief with five Santas

Price Range:
$28-35 either handkerchief in red and green
$15-25 either handkerchief in light blue or pink

3.12 *Description:* Season's Greetings Handkerchief, Welcher

This is a festive linen handkerchief featuring three cats covered in silver stars. The first cat is carrying a candelabrum; the second cat is carrying a small Christmas tree; and the third has both a candelabrum and a small Christmas tree in its paws. They seem to be enjoying the holiday season. This handkerchief has its original J. H. Kimball & Company, Inc. paper label and it is signed Welcher.

Measurements: 15" square
Price Range: $15-18

3.13 *Description:* Embroidered Christmas Guest Towels

These two embroidered guest towels feature poodles enjoying the Christmas holidays. Paragon Needlecraft originally sold these towels as a kit. The patterns were preprinted on the towels and embroidery instruction sheets were included with suggestions for colors of thread and types of embroidery stitches to use. We have seen kits with this pattern dated 1952. Christmas household linen with poodles as subject matter is difficult to find because these items are popular with poodle collectors and Christmas theme collectors.

Measurements: 19"L x 12.75"W
Price Range: $20-30 pair of towels

3.14 *Description:* Christmas Tablecloth

This Christmas tablecloth features poinsettias and candles in the corners, Santa and a Noel banner on two sides, and an angel with a Noel banner on both ends. This tablecloth is similar to many of the vintage Christmas theme tablecloths on the market today.

Measurements: 67"L x 50"W
Price Range: $25-35

4.1 *Description:* Clown with Lute Handkerchief, Carl Tait;
and Harlequin on a Horse Handkerchief, Carl Tait
Carl Tait designed both handkerchiefs. The color
combination on the two linen handkerchiefs is typical of
his work. He often utilized primary colors to create bold
eye-catching designs. The handkerchief above has a few
minor rust stains. The handkerchief to the right is one of
our favorite Tait designs. It was made in at least one other
color combination where the horse is dark green and the
harlequin is primarily mint green. The Herrmann
Handkerchief Company made both handkerchiefs from
Irish linen.
Measurements: 15" square, both handkerchiefs
Price Range:
$30-40 each handkerchief
$15-18 poor condition

The history of the circus dates back to Roman times. In America it began when John Bill Ricketts assembled a troupe of performers in Philadelphia on April 3, 1793. Going to the circus as a child is something most of us fondly remember. The circus is as closely associated with American culture as hot dogs, McDonalds, and Donald Duck. It remains the most enduring form of family entertainment in the world.

When most Americans think of the circus, they think of Ringling Brothers and Barnum & Bailey's *The Greatest Show on Earth*, which has thrilled American audiences since March 29, 1919. Although indoor shows now dominate the business, traveling tented circuses continue to influence the family entertainment business and there are approximately one hundred circus entities in America today.

Most of the collectible circus theme household linen and handkerchiefs found in the marketplace today was made between 1930 and 1960. All of the examples we have in our collections and almost all the pieces we see are fun designs. The typical circus performers are clowns, jugglers, acrobats, and aerialists. Elephants, horses, and lions are the most popular circus animals. The circus is fun and textile designers of the 20th century portrayed the circus as it was because it did not need to be embellished. An exception would be the items with cocktail themes shown in this chapter. The representations with clowns balancing cocktail glasses (Items 4.5 and 4.8) are not representative of circus acts.

Examples of household linen with circus designs are difficult to find. There do not appear to be a large number of collectors for circus theme household linen; however, the prices are generally high. This is likely to be the result of limited supply.

Few circus theme handkerchiefs were made for adults in the 20th century and they are not very collectible unless they bear the signature of a famous designer. Tammis Keefe's circus handkerchiefs command the highest prices in today's marketplace. We have seen them sell for as much as $45. The two handkerchiefs by Carl Tait (Item 4.1) are also popular and collectible.

Circus theme children's handkerchiefs are popular but they are not highly collectible at this time. However, circus handkerchief books for children in good condition are scarce and very collectible. The circus train book shown in this chapter (Item 4.3) is collectible and difficult to find in good condition with all of its original handkerchiefs.

4.2 Description: Appliquéd Carousel Horse Cocktail Napkins
Four carousel horse napkins from a set of six are prancing across the bottom of this page. The appliqué work on these napkins is very good. This set of napkins is very collectible.
Measurements: 5"L x 8.75"W
Price Range: $65-75 set of six

4.3 *Description:* Circus Train Tablecloth and *The Greatest Hanky Show on Earth* Children's Handkerchief Book

Four circus trains are riding around the edge of the tablecloth. This is a perfect tablecloth for children's birthday parties, circus theme parties, or other special occasions in children's lives. There is a children's foldout circus train book sitting on top of the tablecloth. The book has six cars, an elephant engine, and a caboose. Each of the cars has a handkerchief inside showing a different circus animal. A close-up of two pages of the book is also shown. This book originally sold at retail for 59 cents. The subject matter for the book and the tablecloth are based on circus history. Circuses traveled on trains in America as early as the 19th century. It is interesting to note that the book is titled *The Greatest Hanky Show on Earth*. The Ringling Brothers and Barnum & Bailey Circus, *The Greatest Show on Earth*, still rides on its own train.

Measurements:
66"L x 51"W, tablecloth
6.6"L x 49"W, book
Price Range:
$35-45 tablecloth
$50-75 book

4.4 *Description:* Circus Performer Handkerchief, Frederique

This handkerchief signed by Frederique portrays a circus ring with a juggler and a poodle. As mentioned in Chapter 1, poodles were ubiquitous during the "fun linen period." The circus was no exception. We also have this handkerchief in another color combination. The juggler on the second version is performing in a yellow ring and the various items that are colored blue in this photograph have been changed to purple. The second handkerchief has its original paper label that reads "*Bloch Frères*, Linen," indicating the handkerchiefs were made in France.
Measurements: 14.75"L x 15.25"W
Price Range: $18-22

4.5 Description: Acrobatic Clown Bar Towel
Funny acrobatic clowns adorn this colorful towel. The clowns are atypical since
they are balancing cocktail glasses. Circus performers would not ordinarily be
balancing cocktail related items.
Measurements: 30.5"L x 19.5"W
Price Range: $45-60

4.6 Description: Appliquéd Clown Face Cocktail Napkins
Four appliquéd napkins with clown faces are pictured here.
They are from a set of eight napkins. The set consists of two of
each of the napkins shown. It is in mint condition and the
quality of the appliqué is very good. This set is very collectible.
Measurements: 7.75"L x 5"W
Price Range: $75-100 set of eight

4.7 Description: Appliquéd Circus
Cocktail Napkins
Eight oval appliquéd cocktail
napkins with many of the
traditional circus performers and
circus animals are shown here.
The edge of the scalloped border
is machine embroidered. The
quality of the workmanship is very
good. This set of napkins is very
collectible and difficult to find.
Measurements: 4.75"L x 7"W
Price Range: $100-125 set of eight

41

4.8 *Description:* Needle Lace Circus Performer Placemat and Appliquéd Clowns Cocktail Napkins

The appliquéd napkins in this photograph show clowns artfully balancing balls on the tips of their toes. To make it even more difficult, there is a cocktail glass on top of each of the balls. There are eight napkins in this set and all of the napkins have the same scene. The quality of the embroidery on the napkins is very good. They are guaranteed to charm the guests at any cocktail party.

The second item on the page is a very fine needle lace placemat. It is entirely hand made and has a very unusual motif. It is the only needle lace placemat with a circus scene we have seen. Traditional figural themes made of lace are usually gods and goddesses, mythological creatures, courting couples, or hunting scenes. The details in this placemat are wonderful. Even the little poodle balancing a ball on his nose exemplifies the excellent detail. This item is rare and highly collectible.

Measurements:
7"L x 4.5"W, napkins
11"L x 16.875"W, placemat
Price Range:
$65-75 set of eight napkins
$175-225 one placemat

4.9 *Description:* Children's Chenille Bedspread
The vibrant colors in this children's chenille bedspread are wonderful. The pink elephant with his three balloons must have brought smiles to many children's faces over the years. Chenille bedspreads are currently very collectible. They are currently being reproduced and the buyer should be careful when purchasing them.
Measurements: 64"L x 44"W
Price Range: $40-65

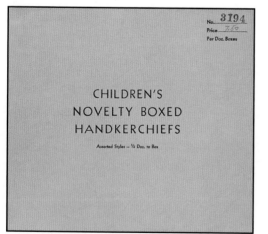

4.10 *Description:* Salesman's Handkerchief Sample Book
The cover of this book indicates that it contains children's novelty handkerchiefs, which were sold in assorted styles. There are two pages with pull-tabs inside the cover. Each page has six handkerchiefs. The left page shows the attractions in Toy Town and advertises admission for ten cents. There are many attractions in Toy Town and three of them, the monkey, the jack-in-the-box, and the children on the seesaw, move when the tab is pulled. There are six clowns on the page of the book to the right. All the clowns except the one eating a row of hot dogs move when the right tab is pulled. This book was created to sell handkerchiefs to retail outlets and it is rare.
Measurements: 11.25"L x 38.25"W
Price Range: $200-225

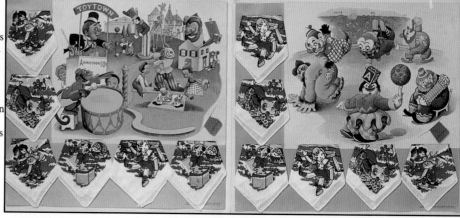

42

4.11 *Description:* Appliquéd Circus Lady Cocktail Napkins
Four appliquéd napkins with ladies performing at the circus are seen here, along with a circus poster from *The Clyde Beatty Cole Brothers Circus*. Circus ladies are a prominent part of circus life. So, not surprisingly, they featured prominently on circus themed household linen from the "fun linen period." The set of eight napkins has two of each scene shown. The ladies have padded breasts and derrières This set of napkins is difficult to find.
Measurements: 6.5"L x 5"W
Price Range: $50-60 set of eight

I tried all I knew her to please,—
But never could please her one quarter so
— well —
As The Man on the Flying Tra-peze!"

One night I, as usual, went to her dear home,
Found there her mother and father alone,
I asked for my love, and soon they made known
To my horror, that she'd run away.

Twas of no avail; she went there ev'ry night
And would throw him bouquets on the stage
She caused him to meet her; and invite her
To tell you would take a whole page. — In-

His movements were graceful
All girls he could please
And my love he purloined
a-way.

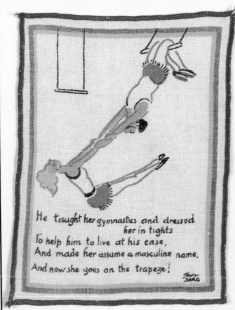

He taught her gymnastics and dressed her in tights
To help him to live at his ease,
And made her assume a masculine name,
And now she goes on the trapeze!

While her time was spent with the Circus Freaks
The tears would roll down like rain from my cheeks
Betrayed by a maid in her teens!

4.12 *Description:* Cocktail Napkins, Tony Sarg
This set of six napkins designed by Tony Sarg tells a sad tale. The gentleman courting the lady on the first napkin loses his love to the man on the flying trapeze. This set portrays a cautionary tale of what can happen when the circus comes to town. If there were a sequel to this set, it would probably show a sadder but wiser young lady returning after weeks of circus life, which is not glamorous. Circus performers with traveling tented shows typically work eleven straight months with only a brief amount of time off at Christmas.
Measurements: 7.25"L x 5.5"W
Price Range: $35-45 set of six

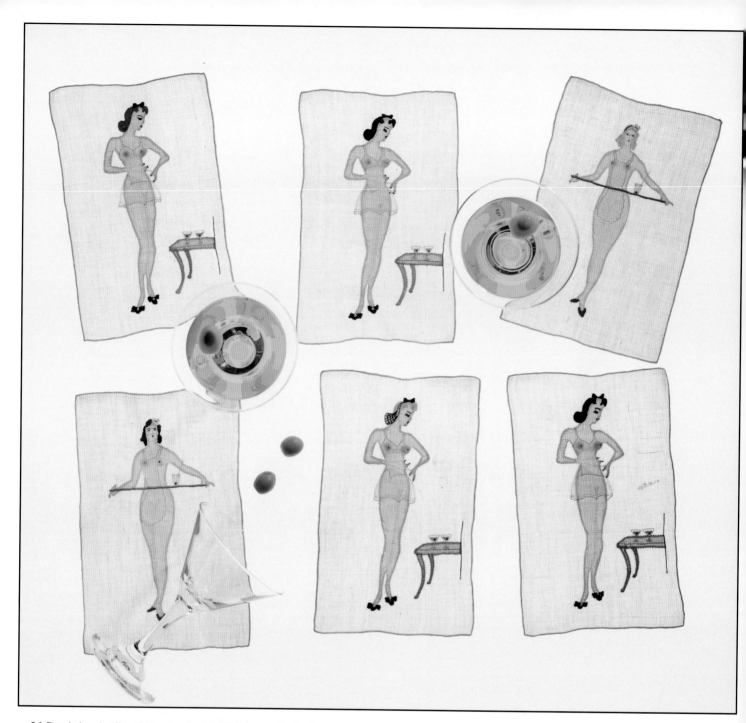

5.1 *Description:* Appliquéd Naughty Ladies With Aprons Cocktail Napkins
Six of the twelve linen napkins in this set are pictured here. The hand-appliquéd
naughty ladies on these napkins are seen serving cocktails clad in see-through frilly
aprons. The ladies were made in two different poses as shown. They also came with
different colors of hair: blonde, brown, and red. The quality of the embroidery is very
good. The napkins are popular collectibles and difficult to find.
Measurements: 8"L x 5"W
Price Range: $125-150 set of twelve

Chapter 5
Cocktails and Spirits

Although there are many anecdotes regarding the precise origin of the word "cocktail," none of them can be documented and experts on the subject believe the true origin of the word has been lost somewhere in the past. The word cocktail first appeared in print in an American newspaper, *Balance and Columbian Repository*, published in Hudson, New York on May 13, 1806. Regardless of the origin of the word, experts agree the cocktail was an American invention.

We have recounted our favorite story regarding the origin of the cocktail below. It should be noted that we are unable to confirm its authenticity.

> What we now know as the tap was originally referred to as the cock in 19th century taverns. The last of the tap was called its tail. As the story goes, Colonel Carter of Culpeper Court House, Virginia, was served the tail of the cock at his local tavern. Not satisfied with it, he dashed it on the floor and exclaimed, "Hereafter I will drink cocktails of my own brewing!" The concoction he then brewed was a combination of gin, lemon peel, bitters, and sugar. Was this the beginning of the cocktail?

Americans' ongoing fascination with the cocktail may be due in large part to the aura of glamour surrounding it. Throughout the 20th century, cocktails have symbolized sophistication. Indeed, the debonair James Bond, ordering his martini "shaken, not stirred," was one of the most enduring figures of the second half of the 20th century.

In the early part of the 20th century, cocktails were primarily associated with the upper classes. They were in vogue at the most fashionable clubs in America where the rich congregated, according to John Hammond Moore, author of *The Cocktail: Our Contribution of Humanity's Salvation*. Moore further states that cocktails were rejected in saloons and pubs at the time. The preferred beverages of the working and lower classes were beer, wine, and straight drinks. During Prohibition people flocked to speakeasies, private clubs, and they frequently served alcohol in their homes. They were drawn by the allure of something risky and forbidden. An interesting phenomenon occurred at this time. People from disparate classes came together to drink. This was the "golden age" of the cocktail.

After Prohibition the cocktail lost some of its appeal. Then, during the Depression cocktails were again a luxury enjoyed only by the wealthiest classes and apparently presidents. Herbert Hoover, the President of the United States from 1928 to 1932, described the cocktail hour as, "The pause between the errors and trials of the day and the hopes of the night."

Most of the fun household linen with cocktails as subject matter was produced after World War II through the 1970s. The demand for cocktail linen during this time period was driven by a postwar cultural environment, which produced the "Organization Man" and Levittown. It was a time of prosperity with a pronounced shift toward more casual dining and entertaining. Hide-a-bars began to appear in the recreation rooms of suburban homes. The cocktail rose in popularity with the middle class. Serving cocktails before dinner became a sign of suburban sophistication.

The cocktail napkins, tablecloths, bar towels, and aprons produced to complement the new suburban lifestyle in America appeared in every theme imaginable: naughty ladies, drunken animals, and inebriated people were all recurring themes. A great deal of the household linen reveals the lifestyle changes that were occurring during the "fun linen period." It should be noted that many of the sentiments expressed on the linens reflect the societal mind-set at the time they were made. By today's standards, many of those sentiments are politically incorrect.

Drinking cocktails was often associated with smoking, since both activities were linked to an image of fashion, sophistication, and women's independence in popular culture in 20th century America. In the 1920s, Lucky Strike produced the first cigarette ads specifically targeting female smokers. These early ads equated smoking with fashionable thinness. The popular slogan "Reach for a Lucky instead of a sweet" actually implied that smoking was beneficial for a woman's health since it dulled the appetite and helped to control one's weight. Virginia Slims launched another famous advertising campaign that encouraged women to smoke in 1968. Who can forget the Virginia Slims ad picturing slender models dressed in the latest fashions with the slogan "You've come a long way, baby"? It is not surprising that smoking motifs featuring women appear on cocktail linens made during the 20th century. We have included an example of a set of smoking motif cocktail napkins depicting a woman's lips with a cigarette (Item 5.2) and an example of a tablecloth showing women smoking at a fashionable party (Item 5.4).

5.2 Description: Embroidered Cigarette Cocktail Napkins
This set of light gray cocktail napkins with embroidered red ruby lips smoking a cigarette is very unusual. One napkin from a set of eight napkins is shown. The embroidery is good quality. These cocktails napkins are reminiscent of a time when smoking was socially acceptable.
Measurements: 7.75"L x 5.25"W
Price Range: $28-36 set of eight

The use of global themes on cocktail napkins, towels, and tablecloths is another interesting design trend to observe in this chapter. Americans were beginning to "spread their wings" during the mid-20th century. This was the era when the legendary Juan Trippe launched the first around the world air service with his flagship airline, Pan American World Airways. Pan Am was considered an extension of American influence throughout the world.

Cocktail themes also appeared on numerous printed handkerchiefs in the mid-20th century. Most of these handkerchiefs had recipes for various types of cocktails. Examples of this type of handkerchief are included in this chapter. We also have a very interesting handkerchief (Item 5.23) that gives advice on how to cure a hangover.

It is not surprising that a number of women's handkerchiefs were designed with cocktail themes since women played a major role in popularizing the cocktail in America. At the same time as Prohibition was forcing consumption of alcohol into homes and private clubs, women were being admitted to private clubs as a result of the suffragist and women's movements. Women popularized cocktails in clubs, which had formerly been exclusively men's drinking places.

Other chapters in this text also have excellent examples of cocktail related items. Of all the themes presented herein, cocktail related items and napkins in particular are probably the most collectible fun textiles of the 20th century.

5.4 Description: Cocktail Party Tablecloth
Look twice! At first glance the scenes on this tablecloth appear to portray a very ordinary black tie cocktail party. The guests are dancing, smoking, playing cards, and relaxing while the host is making drinks with his fashionable cocktail shaker. There is just one thing that seems out of character. One of the guests is dancing with the maid.
Measurements: 35"L x 33.5"W
Price Range: $90-125

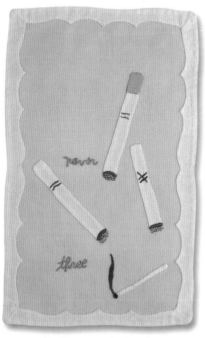

5.3 Description: Never Three Appliquéd Cocktail Napkins
This set of hand-appliquéd cocktail napkins has an unusual motif. The origin of the superstitious saying "never three" comes from World War II. Soldiers lighting cigarettes while sitting in the trenches discovered that the third man on a lighted match was unlucky. When the first soldier lit the match, it would alert enemy snipers. The second man to use the match would allow the snipers to fix the range to the target. By the time the third soldier took the match, the sniper could squeeze the trigger and the enemy fire might hit the unfortunate third man.
Measurements: 8.125"L x 5"W
Price Range: $45-50 set of eight

5.5 Description: Stepping Out Cocktail Napkins
This set of six napkins is machine embroidered. The lady and the gentleman who are part of the set appear to be ready to go out for a formal evening. He will be wearing his top hat and gloves. It appears she will be wearing a tuxedo top. The car is ready and waiting for them. The first time we saw this set we thought it was incomplete. After finding a second set with exactly the same pieces, we concluded it was complete. The top hat the lady is wearing in the photograph is from the second set of napkins. The paper label on the second set reads "Handmade in the Philippines Exclusively for BALOS, 60% Ramie, 40% polyester."
Measurements:
8"L x 4.125"W, hand
8"L x 4.25"W, man's head
6.75"L x 4.5"W, lady's head
4.5"L x 7.125"W, car
7"H x 6"W, hat
7.25"L x 5.5"W, vest
Price Range: $45-55 set of six

5.6 Description: Alphabet Bar Towel, Lois Long

This unusual linen towel signed by Lois Long has eight parts of a man's brain assigned letters corresponding to a wall chart listing different types of liquor such as A for Rye, B for Brandy. Another wall chart lists the tried and true cure for a hangover: take two aspirin every four hours. Just imagine the possibilities if we really did know which type of liquor worked best on each part of the brain. This towel would make a humorous conversation piece at any party.
Measurements: 28"L x 16"W
Price Range: $20-25

5.7 Description: No Wolves Allowed Bar Towel
The sign on the bar says, "No wolves allowed." Apparently, a very fashionably dressed wolf was admitted by mistake. The label on the towel reads "A P & S Creation by the makers of Perma-Kleen tablecloths."
Measurements: 28.25"L x 16"W
Price Range: $25-28

5.8 Description: A Night On The Town Bar Towel
The ladies and the gentlemen on this towel seem to be having a night on the town. Many of the popular drinks served in the United States in the 1940s and 1950s are represented on the towel along with numerous "tipsy" men and women. Very cute little dancing pigs form the border. A companion towel with elephants on the border and graphics of two additional alcoholic beverages, the sidecar and scotch, was featured in an article on collecting dish towels in the June 2001 issue of Martha Stewart's magazine, *Living.*
Measurements: 22.5"L x 14"W
Price Range: $35-45

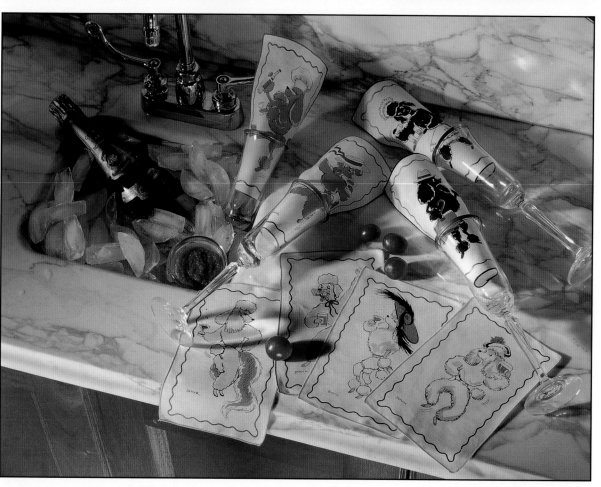

5.9 *Description:* Poodle Cocktail Napkins, Constance Depler
This amusing set of eight poodle napkins signed Depler features a different poodle with a drink in its hand on each napkin. Four of the poodles are masculine and four are feminine. This set is another excellent example of anthropomorphic design. There is a poodle carrying a briefcase on one napkin and another with a feather boa. The slight yellowing from long-term storage will probably disappear when the napkins are washed. It should not affect the price. Poodle motif cocktail napkins are very desirable and typically command high prices in today's marketplace.
Measurements: 8"L x 5.25"W
Price Range: $70-80 set of eight

5.10 *Description:* Figural Poodle Cocktail Napkins
The gray poodle pictured here is looking longingly at the other poodles having a champagne party in the photograph above. Some poodles have all the fun! This set of napkins is very difficult to find.
Measurements: 8"L x 5"W
Price Range: $75-100 set of eight

5.11 *Description:* Appliquéd Elephants and Appliquéd Pigs Cocktail Napkins
The four appliquéd elephant theme napkins are from a set of eight, which includes two napkins with each of the scenes shown. The napkins still have their original paper labels stating they are "Linen, Hand Embroidered with Cotton, Madeira, Portugal." Embroidered elephants are unusual motifs for cocktail napkins. Printed pink elephants are more common. The four pig napkins are from a set of eight napkins, which includes two each of the napkin designs as shown. The napkins are hand embroidered and trimmed with a small piece of crochet along one edge. They still have their original paper labels stating they are "Linen Cotton Decorations Madeira Portugal." Cocktail napkins with pig motifs are very collectible and difficult to find. All the napkins in this set have yellowed after having been stored for many years in a cardboard box. This type of uniform yellowing is easily removed when the items are washed. It should not affect the price.
Measurements:
8.25"L x 5.25"W, elephants
5"L x 7.75"W, pigs
Price Range:
$125-135 set of eight pigs
$50-60 set of eight elephants

5.12 Description: Bartender Placemat Set
A tribute to those who drink beer! This machine-embroidered set consists of six placemats with matching napkins and a runner. The set has two different scenes: a bartender serving foamy mugs of beer and a waiter carrying a tray filled with full beer mugs. Cheerful and inexpensive, this type of set is very useful for casual entertaining. We have added this set to acknowledge the popularity of beer in America. In spite of its popularity, a very limited amount of fun household linen with beer as the subject matter was made in the 20th century.
Measurements:
15" square, napkins
10.75"L x 15"W, placemats
33"L x 16.5"W, runner
Price Range: $35-40 thirteen-piece set

5.13 Description: Scottish Terrier Lipstick Towel
The Scottish Terrier on this lipstick towel is enjoying a drink in a glass almost as large as he. This lipstick hand towel is a perfect addition to a powder room for evenings when guests will be invited for cocktails.
Measurements: 12"L x 8.25"W
Price Range: $15-18

5.14 Description: Cocktail Waitress Bar Towel
The cute cocktail waitress is printed on the bottom right-hand side of this bar towel. She seems to need more practice balancing her tray above her head. Her cocktails are on their way to the floor.
Measurements: 24"L x 16.5"W
Price Range: $18-25

5.15 Description: Mountain Boy Napkins, Paul Webb
Six pieces are shown from a set of eight cocktail napkins featuring hillbilly cartoons. The set was designed by Paul Webb and printed on handkerchief-type material. The napkins came in the brown jug shaped folder, which is also pictured on this page. This set was also made in green.
Measurements: 7"L x 5"W
Price Range:
$30-35 set of eight
$25-30 set of eight without the folder

5.16 Description: Pink Elephant Apron, Tony Sarg

Tony Sarg designed this wonderful and rare apron circa 1930. The elephants on the apron are preparing drinks. They bear a distinct resemblance to the fun-loving elephant on one of the Sarg cocktail napkins on the adjoining page (Item 5.18). *Tony Sarg's Book of Animals* also appears on this page. The book was published in 1925. The illustrations in the book and on the apron portray remarkable anthropomorphic designs. Household linen designed by Tony Sarg is very collectible. Because Sarg was also a puppeteer, illustrator, and author, many people who purchase other collectibles he designed or illustrated (toys, puppets, books) also purchase his household linen. This increases the number of potential buyers for his textile designs, which are scarce.

Measurements: 35.5"L x 31"W
Price Range: $100-125

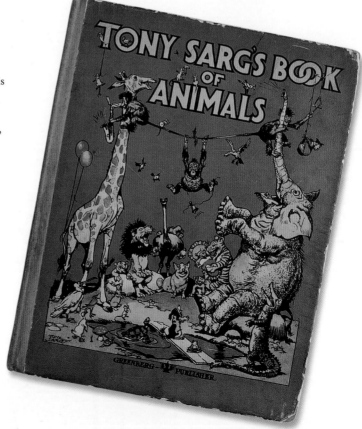

5.17 Description: Pink Elephant Bar Towel
Pink elephants holding various types of drinks are cavorting throughout this linen towel. The subject matter makes this towel highly collectible.
Measurements: 28"L x 14.5"W
Price Range: $40-45

5.18 Description: Fantasy Cocktail Napkins, Tony Sarg
This set of eight cocktail napkins is another excellent example of anthropo-morphic design by Tony Sarg. It was originally sold in a circus-inspired gift box with matching cork coasters. The set is circa 1930. It is very collectible and difficult to find.
Measurements: 7.25"L x 5"W
Price Range: $125-150 set of eight

51

5.19 Description: Bottom's Up Bar Towel
Cocktail glasses are dancing, singing, and playing on the towel shown here. The glasses, having assumed human form, are each holding a different drink. All of the dancing glasses are represented in the napkin set (Item 5.20) seen below. This is the first example of a global theme represented on cocktail linen in this chapter.
Measurements: 28"L x 15.75"W
Price Range: $28-35

5.20 Description: Bottom's Up Cocktail Napkins Folder
The eight napkins in this Leacock & Company, Inc. folder have the same patterns as the towel shown above printed on them. Most of the drinks represented on the napkins and the towel with the exception of the Cuba Libre are still popular in America. The Cuba Libre is a classic Cuban drink, which America adopted as its own in the 1930s. The folder reads "Leacock, Cocktail set, Bottom's Up." This set of napkins is another example of the global themes prevalent on cocktail themed textiles during the "fun linen period."
Measurements: 8.5"L x 5.5"W, napkins
Price Range: $45-65 set of eight

5.21 Description: International Bar Handkerchief
Toasts in various languages are printed on this handkerchief. Interesting cocktail motif handkerchiefs are currently quite popular with collectors. This handkerchief is difficult to find and very collectible.
Measurements: 12"L x 12.25"W
Price Range: $40-45

5.22 Description: Cocktail Recipes Handkerchief
This handkerchief is sprinkled with various drink recipes that seem particularly well suited to the people featured. The newly married couple with the bride clutching a drink called "Maiden's Prayer" is absolutely priceless. This is another very collectible and difficult to find cocktail motif handkerchief.
Measurements: 11.375"L x 11.625"W
Price Range: $40-45

5.23 Description: How to Cure a Hangover Handkerchief, *Desin Deposé*
This colorful French handkerchief lists various remedies for a hangover. It is signed *Desin Deposé* in one corner. After reading some of the remedies, we decided the cure would be worse than the hangover!
Measurements: 20.5" square
Price Range: $45-50

5.24 *Description:* Painted Lady Cocktail Napkins and Printed Bar Towel

There are eight painted cocktail napkins with ladies dressed in afternoon attire in this set. Six napkins from the set are shown. The subject matter on each napkin is a lady with an unusual hat holding a drink. Actually, unusual may be the wrong word for four of the hats. They may be more aptly described as bizarre! The lady in the green polka dot dress is wearing a hat in the shape of a birdcage with a bird sitting in it. There are birds kissing on the top of another hat, and a mother bird feeding her young on a third hat. The fourth bizarre hat is on the lady with the red, white, and blue outfit. Her hat has an odd eagle wearing a hat and holding an American flag.

A very interesting bar towel is pictured opposite the ladies. There are people dancing on the towel and holding recipes for various drinks. Most of the liquor and the bar accessories needed to make the drinks are also represented on the towel. The edge of the towel has pink elephants marching in a row with their trunks up. The contrast between the subject matter on the towel and the napkins is noteworthy. The napkins portray drinking in a sophisticated setting, and the towel portrays it as a way of relaxing and letting down your hair. Again, we see the global theme portrayed on the towel.
Measurements:
9.5" square, napkins
26.5"L x 17"W, towel
Price Range:
$75-100 set of eight napkins
$25-35 towel

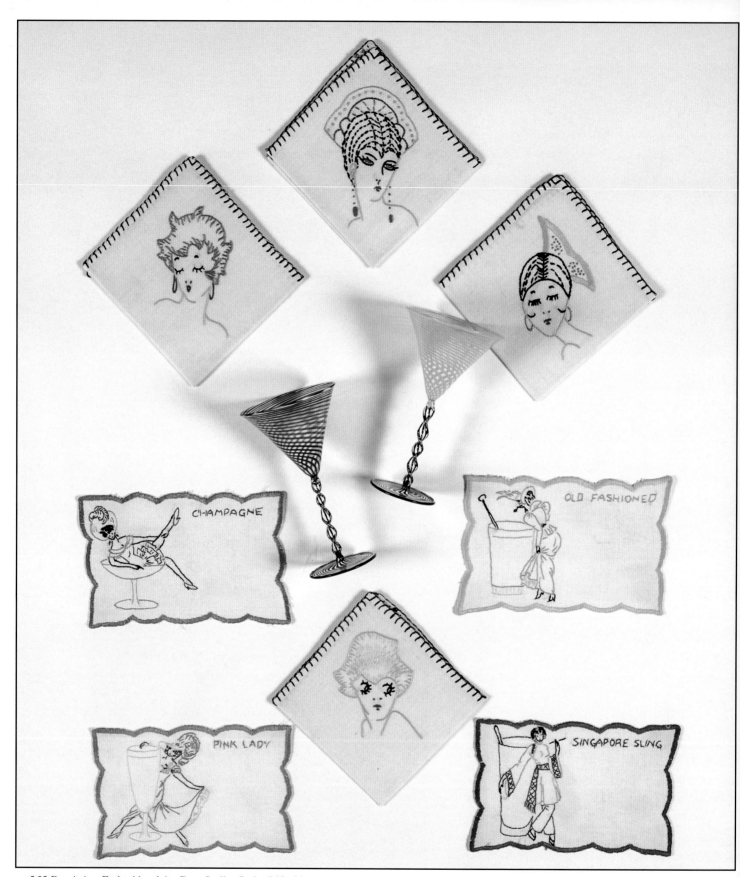

5.25 Description: Embroidered Art Deco Ladies Cocktail Napkins
There are two sets of napkins shown. The four napkins with art deco ladies' faces were hand embroidered. This set is unusual and we have not seen another example. The second set of napkins was made for commercial sale. The edges of this set of eight napkins are machine stitched and the ladies are hand embroidered. There are two of each of the napkins shown in the set.
Measurements:
9.5"L x 10"W, art deco ladies' faces napkins
4 .125"L x 6.5"W, ladies and glasses napkins
Price Range:
$45-65 art deco ladies' faces, set of four
$35-45 ladies and glasses, set of eight

5.26 Description: Cocktail Napkins, Fabrés
The set of eight printed linen cocktail napkins is signed by Fabrés. Each napkin features a different type of liquor and a person often associated with each type of drink. There is a pirate with his rum and a Scotsman in a kilt playing bagpipes with an amazing scotch bottle wearing a matching kilt running alongside him. This set of napkins is in poor condition: two of the napkins have holes or tears.
Measurements: 8.25"L x 5.5"W
Price Range:
$55-60 set of eight
$30-36 set of eight, poor condition

5.27 Description: Global Cocktail Recipes Tablecloth and Cocktail Napkin Folder
This tablecloth and napkin set is by Dervan and shows a global theme. There are recipes for drinks and dancing people around the border of the tablecloth. Each drink recipe has one or more costumed people dancing in the middle of it. The center portion of the tablecloth has two champagne bottles surrounded by grapes and various names of drinks printed on it. The drink recipes on this towel have their origins in many countries. Some of the drinks represented are La France, Gripsholm Speciale, and Hawaiian Special. (This tablecloth predates Hawaiian statehood, which did not occur until 1959.) There are six napkins in the matching folder, which reads "Global Gaities, Cocktail Set" on the cover and "Linens by Dervan" on the back. Each napkin features a drink recipe that matches one of the recipes on the tablecloth.
Measurements:
36"L x 32"W, tablecloth
8.5"L x 5.5"W, napkins
Price Range:
$35-45 tablecloth
$35-45 set of six napkins

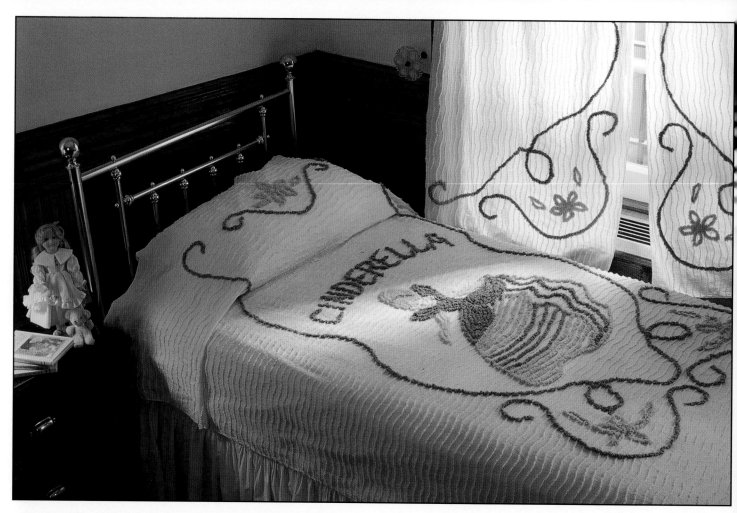

6.1 *Description:* Chenille *Cinderella* Bedspread and Curtains
Cinderella is one of the best-known fairy tales of all time. It has inspired countless books and movies. Variations of this fairy tale appear in many different cultures. The earliest recorded version was written in China in the 9th century. Disney's *Cinderella* inspired the bedspread and curtains shown in this photograph. Cinderella is seen in the center of the bedspread dressed in a beautiful ball gown. There is scrollwork around her, and three flowers are embroidered on the bedspread at the bottom left and right-hand corners and top center. One set of matching chenille curtains from a set of two is shown. The curtains have a scroll pattern similar to the bedspread and each has an embroidered flower on one corner. Chenille curtains are very difficult to find. As a result, this set along with the bedspread is very rare. We recently saw a similar set of curtains (81"L x 32"W) without the bedspread sell at auction for $330.
Measurements:
88"L x 68"W, bedspread
64"L x 37"W, curtains
Price Range: $175-225

6.2 *Description: A Hanky-A-Day Mother Goose Book*
This children's handkerchief book folds out to show illustrations from various nursery rhymes. There are seven pages with rhymes, and a total of nine pages plus the cover. There is a child's handkerchief on each of the nursery rhyme pages. The book is called *A Hanky-A-Day Mother Goose Book*. The back cover has "A Julian S. Cohn Creation U.S.A" printed on it. Days of the week handkerchief books were very popular in the "fun linen period." A very limited number of books with fairy tale themes were produced.
Measurements: 9.25"L x 50"W
Price Range: $75-100

Chapter 6

Fairy Tales, Nursery Rhymes, and Proverbs

Fairy tales, nursery rhymes, and proverbs were very popular in America as well as many other countries throughout the 20th century. There are fairy tales from almost all cultures of the world and it is interesting to note that variations of many of the most famous tales from western cultures also appear in many other cultures. For example, from countries with cultures as seemingly disparate as China and Egypt we find fairy tales very similar in content to *Cinderella*. Perhaps these tales are so popular because most people, regardless of their cultural backgrounds, are attracted to stories about living happily ever after, good winning over evil, and the power of love, all of which are common themes in fairy tales.

Any discussion of fairy tales in 20th century America would be incomplete without mentioning Walt Disney Productions. Although the most popular fairy tales of all time did not originate in America, this country is now strongly associated with the Disney versions of many of these tales. This is due to numerous animated films made and distributed worldwide by Disney during the 20th century, including: *Snow White and the Seven Dwarfs*, *Sleeping Beauty*, *Cinderella*, and *Pinocchio*.

Walt Disney Productions had an enormous impact on the American economy as early as the 1920s when its first cartoon, *Steamboat Willie*, was released and Disney began to license Mickey Mouse and Mickey related products worldwide. In 1937, Disney's production of its first full-length animated film based on the classic fairy tale, *Snow White and the Seven Dwarfs*, was actually credited with helping "jump start" the depressed American economy. Although many doubted that the movie would succeed because it cost the then unheard of total of two million dollars to produce, it went on to become one of the best selling movies of all time. *The New York Times* reported Disney's success in an article in its May 2, 1938, edition that stated: "117 toy manufacturers have been licensed to use characters from *Snow White*. The only thing in the picture that the public doesn't seem to crave is poisoned apples." *Snow White's* overwhelming success inspired the development of a new industry from its by-products. A number of American companies that

were failing during the Depression suddenly began to recover as a result. Industrialized fantasy had become big business in America and fairy tales were part of this business.

Walt Disney's animated film classics based on well-known fairy tales inspired a number of children's handkerchief and household linen designs during the "fun linen period." The children's chenille bedspread and curtain set pictured on the opposite page is an example of Disney's influence on household linen. This set was inspired by the Disney film version of *Cinderella*, which was first released in 1950. In addition, the following items were also likely to have been inspired by Disney: the appliquéd *Snow White and the Seven Dwarfs* tablecloth (Item 6.12); the *Pinocchio* children's tablecloth and napkin set (Item 6.13); and the *Sleeping Beauty* embroidery kit manufactured by a company licensed by Disney (Item 6.14).

6.3 Description: Leprechaun Cocktail Napkins
There are two different scenes portrayed on this set of ten linen napkins. One napkin from each scene is shown. The leprechaun sitting under a fruit tree is a combination of appliqué and satin stitch while the "tipsy" fellow under the table is made entirely with satin stitch. Leprechauns are loved creatures since they usually find their way into fairy tale lore as small creatures who know where the pot of gold is hidden at the end of the rainbow. Napkins and other household linen featuring these fairy tale creatures are very unusual. The unusual motif makes this set quite desirable.
Measurements: 5.5"L x 7"W
Price Range: $30-35 set of ten

Nursery rhyme textiles are also found in this chapter. Before the 19th century, nursery rhymes were referred to as "ditties" or "songs." It is likely that they were originally part of tavern songs, folk songs, ballads, proverbs, political satires, and even prayers. In their earliest forms, the overwhelming majority of nursery rhymes were not intended to entertain children. However, by the 20th century nursery rhymes were very much a part of the lives of American children. The nursery rhyme book pictured as Item 6.2 is an interesting example of a gift of handkerchiefs and nursery rhymes for children. Seven classic nursery rhymes are included in the book along with a different handkerchief for each day of the week.

In a similar fashion to fairy tales, nursery rhymes are also common in many other cultures. *The Oxford Dictionary of Nursery Rhymes* mentions that "*Humpty Dumpty* of England is elsewhere known as *Boule, boule* (France), *Thille Lille* (Sweden), *Lille-Trille* (Denmark), *Hillerin-Lillerin* (Finland), *Annebadadeli* (Switzerland), and *Trille Trölle, Etje-Papetje, Wirgele-Wargele, Gigele-Gagele, Rüntzelken-Püntzelken,* and *Hümpelken-Pümpelken* (different parts of Germany)." Humpty Dumpty was a popular figure on 20th century children's handkerchiefs and we have included an example of a Tom Lamb handkerchief that features Humpty Dumpty and other well-known nursery rhyme characters (Item 6.9) in this chapter.

Some textiles from the "fun linen period" depict modern versions of old nursery rhymes. The handkerchief pictured as Item 6.10 is an amusing 1950s interpretation of the 19th century *Old Mother Hubbard* nursery rhyme while the towel in Item 6.15 shows a butler doing the shopping in a 20th century rendition of *To Market, to Market,* a rhyme that originated in the 16th century.

Proverbs

Proverbs are brief well-known sayings that are self-evident (common sense). Although we have included an example of a proverb handkerchief (Item 6.16) and a set of napkins (Item 6.17) in this chapter, we actually have very few examples in our collections. Textiles with proverbs as subject matter are not plentiful. This is surprising since proverbs are very much a part of our everyday lives.

Almost all of us were raised with fairy tales, nursery rhymes, and proverbs. Even the tremendous impact of television did not take away the tradition of reading and reciting them to children. Textiles with fairy tales, nursery rhymes, and proverbs were evident throughout the century. Fairy tales and nursery rhymes were very popular themes on printed handkerchiefs and towels but not on tablecloths. Nursery rhymes were also popular themes on embroidered days of the week towel sets and children's bedspreads. However, they are not commonly found in any other types of embroidered 20th century household linen. Among the items featured in this chapter, the children's handkerchiefs and the *Cinderella* bedspread and curtains are currently the most desirable collectibles.

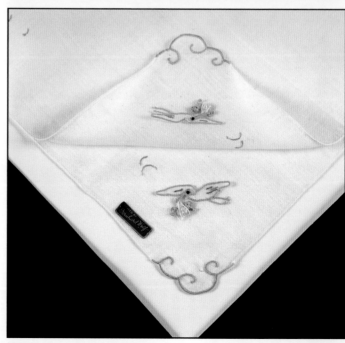

Opposite page, top to bottom:

6.4 Description: Sleeping Beauty *Handkerchief*
The tale of *Sleeping Beauty* goes back to an Arthurian romance, *Perceforest*, which was first published in 1528. This textile version was made in the first quarter of the 20th century. It shows two scenes from the fairy tale. The bottom scene shows the king and queen being informed of the miracle and the top scene shows the prince awakening his love.
Measurements: 12"L x 12.5"W
Price Range: $75-90

6.5 Description: Fairy Tale Tablecloth
This 1950s fairy tale tablecloth features a wealth of different figures throughout. There are kings, queens, princesses, castles, goblins, mermaids, and other interesting characters on this piece. The characters remind us of Grimm's fairy tales. The tablecloth has vibrant color and excellent detail.
Measurements: 48"L x 56"W
Price Range: $45-60

6.6 Description: Madeira Stork Handkerchief
This is an amusing hand-embroidered rendition of the folk tale about storks delivering babies. The middle of each of the storks is attached to the handkerchief and the wings can be lifted up. Note the little baby in diapers being carried by the storks in two of the handkerchief's corners. The handkerchief retains its two original paper labels that read "Styled by Bernhard Wolf" and "Hand Made in Madeira, Portugal." The original price tag from Strawbridge and Clothier is also attached. It reads "59 cents."
Measurements: 11.75"L x 12"W
Price Range: $25-28

Right, top to bottom:

6.7 Description: Appliquéd Tablecloth
Fairies have existed in mythology and folklore for countless centuries. However, they have never been a widely used motif for textile designs. This lavender colored linen tablecloth is one of the earliest examples in this chapter. It dates to the art deco period when nymphs and fairies were very popular. The fairies are done in black cotton fabric and applied by hand. There are hand-embroidered trees and branches on the cloth with French knot flowers. The quality of the embroidery is very good and the tablecloth is rare. We have not seen another example of this design.
Measurements: 34.5" square
Price Range: $50-65

6.8 Description: The Tortoise and the Hare *Handkerchief, Pat Prichard*
Pat Prichard signed this linen handkerchief. Based on a story from Aesop's Fables, it shows the race between the slow and steady tortoise and the swift but extremely busy hare. Between eating carrots, picking flowers, taking a nap, courting his sweetheart, and reading a book, this was one busy hare! No wonder the much slower but steadier tortoise was able to win the race. This handkerchief is difficult to find in mint condition. It retains its original yellow and gold J. H. Kimball & Company, Inc. paper label.
Measurements: 15" square
Price Range: $30-35

6.9 Description: Nursery Rhyme Handkerchief, Tom Lamb
The well-dressed pig in the center of this Tom Lamb children's handkerchief is reading a book of nursery rhymes and fairy tales. Scenes from well-known tales and rhymes are along the border. In one corner we see the big bad wolf and the three little pigs. Humpty Dumpty is on the other corner. In addition, the cow jumping over the moon from *Hey Diddle Diddle*, and the mouse running up the clock from *Hickory, Dickory, Dock* are included on the handkerchief. *Hickory, Dickory, Dock* is a nursery rhyme that traces its origins to an early rhyme used for counting.
Measurements: 9" square
Price Range: $10-$15

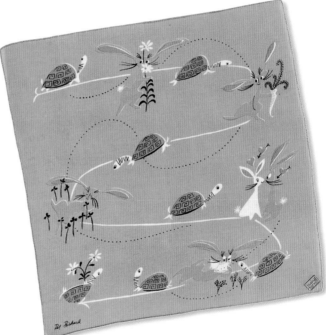

6.10 *Description: Old Mother Hubbard* Handkerchief
Old Mother Hubbard as portrayed on this children's handkerchief has been adapted for the 1950s reader. It is complete with a black poodle! The inspiration for the nursery rhyme on this handkerchief came from the 19th century version of the rhyme in the book *The Comic Adventures of Old Mother Hubbard and Her Dog*, written by Sarah Catherine Martin and published by John Harris in 1805.
Measurements: 9.75"L x 10"W
Price Range: $25-30

6.11 *Description:* Embroidered Nursery Rhyme Towels
Six nursery rhyme characters are hand embroidered on these towels. The embroidery work is very good. Miss Muffet is a particularly interesting rendering with her hair and bowl flying in fear of the spider. This set of towels was made in the last quarter of the 20th century from vintage transfer patterns. Similar vintage sets are available.
Measurements: 34.5"L x 23.5"W
Price Range:
$35-40 sets from the fourth quarter of the century
$75-85 vintage sets

6.12 Description: Snow White and the Seven Dwarfs Tablecloth
In the textile version of *Snow White* shown here, she is seen in the center of the tablecloth with birds flying above her and the seven dwarfs surrounding her. The name of each dwarf is embroidered on his hat. Several of the dwarfs are incorporated into scenes. The scene of Bashful with the deer is particularly cute. Unfortunately, Happy has a damaged outfit and the cloth has been washed extensively; therefore, we consider it to be in poor condition.
Measurements: 32"L x 31"W
Price Range:
$75-100
$25-30 poor condition

6.13 Description: Pinocchio Children's Tablecloth and Napkin Set
This set was likely to have been inspired by the Disney film *Pinocchio*, which was released in 1940. The tablecloth and four napkins are in mint condition. They are made from pieces of printed fabric showing scenes of Pinocchio's adventures. The white border is attached with machine stitches.
Measurements:
30" square, tablecloth
9.5" square, napkins
Price Range: $25-30 five-piece set

6.14 Description: Walt Disney's *Sleeping Beauty* Guest Towels Embroidery Kit
Disney's animated version of *Sleeping Beauty*, based on Charles Perrault's *La Belle au Bois Dormant*, has been delighting audiences around the world since its initial release in 1959. The manufacturer of this kit was licensed by Disney to produce this *Sleeping Beauty* inspired embroidery kit. The manufacturer's name, "Transogram Toys and Games since 1913," is printed on all four corners of the cover. There are six pre-printed towels in this set: two towels show Princess Aurora, two others show Prince Phillip, and the remaining two show the Enchanted Castle. The kit included different colored spools of thread and a sheet of instructions (which is now missing) describing the type of stitches to apply on the various areas of each towel. Instructions on how to do various simple embroidery stitches are on the cover of the box. The quality of the print and the material included with this set indicate it was an inexpensive set. This is not surprising since the kit was clearly intended as a teaching tool for children. The literature on the side of the cover states this set was "designed especially for little girls 5 years and up who love to 'sew like Mommy.' " Unfortunately, the box is in poor condition and a previous owner had begun to embroider two of the towels with a very unskilled hand. This set would be more appealing to Disney memorabilia, toy, or household linen collectors if it had been in an untouched condition.
Measurements: 12"L x 8.75"W, each towel
Price Range:
$60-65 boxed set
$10-15 boxed set, poor condition

6.15 *Description: To Market To Market To Buy A Fat Pig* Towel
The kitchen towel shown is a modern version of the rhyme: *To market, to market, to buy a fat pig, Home again, home again, jiggety-jig; To market, to market, to buy a fat hog, Home Again, home again, jiggety-jog.* The butler has already been to town, birds are flying above, the basket is full of food, and the expression on the butler's face indicates all is well with the world. Earlier graphic versions of this tale usually portray children going to town. The graphics on this towel are excellent.
Measurements: 32"L x 18"W
Price Range: $25-30

6.16 *Description: Rain, Rain Go Away* Handkerchief, Carl Tait
This Irish linen handkerchief signed by Carl Tait is based on an old children's nursery rhyme, *Rain, rain, go away, Come again another day.* The design lends new meaning to several other old sayings: "it's raining cats and dogs" and "it's raining buckets." This handkerchief still has its Herrmann Handkerchief Company triangular silver colored paper label attached.
Measurements: 14.75" square
Price Range: $40-45

6.17 *Description:* Proverbs Cocktail Napkins Folder, Carl Tait
This is a set of eight hand-printed linen cocktail napkins signed by Carl Tait depicting various well-known proverbs. The napkins are still in their original cardboard Leacock & Company, Inc. presentation folder. The copyright date on the folder is 1952. Both the folder and the napkins are in excellent condition. Carl Tait also designed several proverbs handkerchiefs, which are similar to these napkins.
Measurements: 5.25"L x 8.25"W, each napkin
Price Range: $40-45 set of eight napkins in the folder

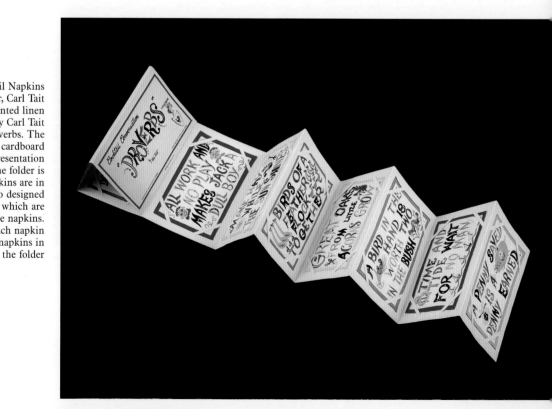

64

6.18 *Description:* Modern *Cinderella* Handkerchief

A very modern interpretation of *Cinderella*, the classic fairy tale, is shown on this handkerchief. This version is very unusual and collectible. Most *Cinderella* designs are either very traditional or based on Walt Disney's *Cinderella*. This design incorporates many of the important elements from the story such as the clock striking midnight, the pumpkin that turned into a coach, and one of the glass slippers that was the key to her living happily ever after with her Prince Charming. The quality of the printing is average and there are several areas where the color was smudged and/or did not quite stay within the black outlines. Another handkerchief in this series features *Sleeping Beauty*.

Measurements: 14.75"L x 15"W
Price Range: $12-15

7.1 Description: Appliquéd Delphinium Placemats, Napkins, and a Runner, Marghab

The four placemats and the runner shown above are made of Margandie, a very fine organdy, and the napkins are made of very fine linen. Delphinium is one of the finest Marghab designs. It was a very difficult and expensive design to produce. Consequently, a very limited number of items in this pattern are available in the marketplace today. All the embroidery was done by hand. The reader should note the incredible level of detail in each floral stalk. The leaves are all hand appliqué. This pattern was one of three Marghab patterns selected by the Metropolitan Museum of Art for display.

Measurements:
16.5"L x 16.875"W, each napkin
11.5"L x 17"W, each placemat
36"L x 11.5"W, runner
Price Range: $800-900 nine-piece set

66

People the world over love flowers. In America as in other countries, flowers are often used for celebrations and given as gifts for birthdays, Valentine's Day, anniversaries, graduations, and many other celebratory occasions. Therefore, it is not surprising that flowers were the most popular motif on 20th century household linen and handkerchiefs. Although sizes, shapes, and colors changed over the decades, flowers remained the 20th century's favorite subject matter for household linen and handkerchiefs.

Representations of flowers on household linen from the early part of the century were typically white or pastel in color and resembled flowers in their natural state. During the "fun linen period" designers began to produce fantasy flower patterns in clashing shades of color similar to the Vera towel pictured as Item 7.9. It is interesting to note that unlike most other topics in this text, anthropomorphic themes were not common in floral motif fun household linen or handkerchiefs at any point in the 20th century.

Vera Neumann, better known as Vera, was particularly famous for the new wave in floral household linen that surfaced during the mid-20th century. She was probably the most prolific designer of household linen in the third quarter of the 20th century. Tammis Keefe and Luther Travis also designed numerous printed household linen items with floral themes. However, the output of these two designers combined was still exceeded by the total number of floral designs produced by Vera. Of the three designers mentioned above, Vera's floral motif items and her towels in particular are currently the most desirable.

In terms of fun household linen with floral motifs produced in the 20th century, probably the most desirable items in today's marketplace are table linen with very fine embroidery like the Marghab placemat set pictured as Item 7.1. In terms of printed fun household linen, towels and tablecloths are currently the most collectible items. Printed towels and tablecloths, which were designed and signed by famous designers, are usually more desirable to collectors and they command higher prices than unsigned pieces. However, unsigned pieces with unusual designs are also collectible. The zinnia tablecloth (Item 7.13) is an example of a very unusual and collectible unsigned tablecloth.

The majority of handkerchiefs produced for women in the 20th century were floral in theme and very few were signed. The demand for floral handkerchiefs reached its peak during the "fun linen period." To satisfy the consistently strong demand for floral handkerchiefs during this period, manufacturers produced and sold large quantities at very reasonable prices. Floral handkerchiefs were printed or embroidered (both by machine and by hand) and were also sometimes trimmed with lace.

Printed handkerchiefs are becoming popular collectibles. Several books featuring 20th century handkerchiefs have been published over the past few years. In 1998 the Boston Public Library at Copley Square featured an exhibit of floral handkerchiefs from the 1940s and 1950s from Phoebe Ann Erb's collection. Three photographs of displays from this exhibit are featured as Item 7.3. There was also an exhibit in 1999 in Lexington, Massachusetts at the Museum of Our National Heritage on floral handkerchiefs. Phoebe Ann Erb's collection was again featured and she was the guest curator for the exhibit.

Flower shaped and round floral theme handkerchiefs are difficult to find and typically command the highest prices. An excellent example of a flower shaped handkerchief is pictured as Item 7.4.

7.2 Description: Girl Watering Her Garden Children's Handkerchief
The little girl is watering her garden of flowers and fruit. She has managed to grow a wonderful crop of strawberries in the middle of her lovely flowers. The little bug holding a shovel in this scene is clearly intending to help in the garden.
Measurements: 11.25"L x 10.25"W
Price Range: $10-12

Photographer: Ellen Jane Katz   *Photographer: Ellen Jane Katz*   *Photographer: Ellen Jane Katz*

7.3 Description: Sweet Memories: An Exhibit of Printed Handkerchiefs, Boston Public Library, 1998
In the 1940s and the '50s printed handkerchief production was at its peak and floral designs flooded the markets. Handkerchief advertisements often featured a floral design described in flowery language. Anonymous designers dreamed up endless varieties of bouquets, nosegays, garlands, sprays, and all over buds and blossoms in colors to accent any outfit. Stemmer House Books published a compendium of some of these designs, *Floral Designs From Traditional Printed Handkerchiefs* by Phoebe Ann Erb, in 1998. These three photographs are from "Sweet Memories," an exhibit of the collection of Phoebe Ann Erb, which was held at the Boston Public Library in 1998. Phoebe's collection continues to exhibit around the country.

7.4 Description: Daffodil Handkerchief
This is a stunning floral handkerchief. During the "fun linen period," a number of floral motif handkerchiefs were made in the shapes of various flowers such as roses, carnations, orchids, and so forth. This type of handkerchief is very popular with handkerchief collectors today. This example retains its original paper label that reads "Floral Bouquets Styled By Bernhard Wolf, Hand rolled." The original price tag is still stapled on the piece. It reads, "Pries, Norwalk, O., $.49."
Measurements: 13"L x 13.25"W
Price Range: $25-28

7.5 *Description:* Ferns and Wildflowers Tablecloth, Tammis Keefe
Printed linen tablecloths signed by Tammis Keefe are difficult to find. Her tablecloth designs with animals and people are more desirable than her floral themed tablecloths similar to the one pictured here. This tablecloth design is titled "Fern" and was made by Falflax. It was also made with a light blue color in a larger size (72"L). Tammis Keefe also used similar fern and wildflower designs in several of her handkerchief designs.
Measurements: 51"L x 50"W
Price Range: $55-75

7.6 *Description:* Persian Garden Cocktail Napkins, Georges Briard
"Persian Garden" was a popular Georges Briard pattern. In addition to the set of eight napkins pictured here, Briard used this pattern on a number of dinnerware items. He also used it on paper napkins and cups. The flowers on these linen napkins are outlined in metallic gold. The set is in its original box, which is distinctive and decorative. "Cocktail Napkins by Georges Briard, Pure Linen, M. Wille Co. Product" is printed on the box. Georges Briard produced a number of printed cocktail napkins with abstract designs. Many unused sets of his napkins in their original gift boxes are still readily available in the marketplace.
Measurements: 5"L x 6.5"W
Price Range: $30-36 set of eight

7.7 Description: Floral Apron, Vera
This is an attractive linen apron displaying one of Vera's trademark floral designs. There are two little pockets on the bottom left and right corners. Vera typically made kitchen towels to match her aprons and they could be purchased in sets that contained an apron and two matching towels.
Measurements: 16.5"L x 17.5"W gathered at the waist
Price Range: $12-15

7.8 Description: Floral Basket Crocheted Doily
This figural hand-crocheted doily is very unusual. The basket was made and then the flowers and leaves were applied. Similar pieces were often seen in homes on coffee tables and small side tables in the mid-20th century.
Measurements: 14"L x 11"W
Price Range: $12-15

7.9 Description: Flower Power Towel, Vera
Vera was known for her bold flower designs. This towel is best suited to a pop art kitchen of the 1960s.
Measurements: 28.5"L x 16"W
Price Range: $20-25

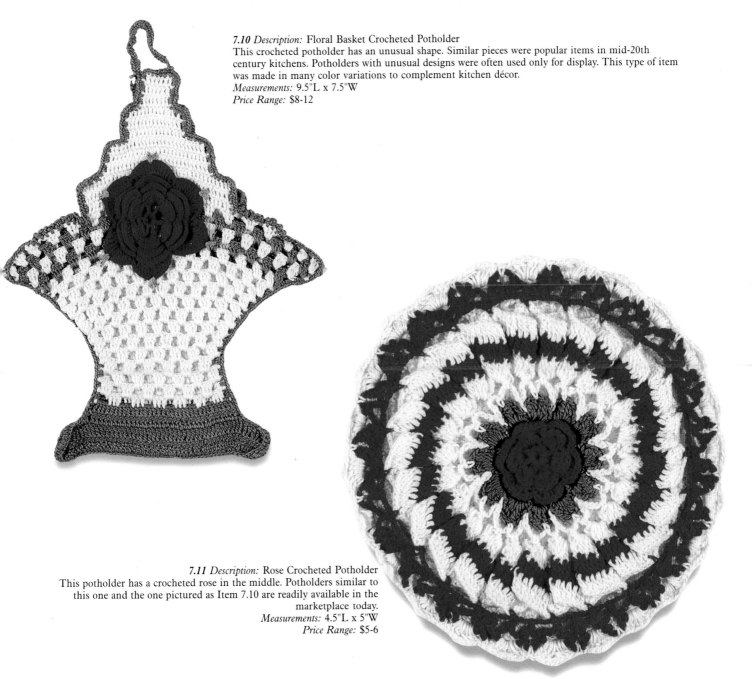

7.10 *Description:* Floral Basket Crocheted Potholder
This crocheted potholder has an unusual shape. Similar pieces were popular items in mid-20th century kitchens. Potholders with unusual designs were often used only for display. This type of item was made in many color variations to complement kitchen décor.
Measurements: 9.5"L x 7.5"W
Price Range: $8-12

7.11 *Description:* Rose Crocheted Potholder
This potholder has a crocheted rose in the middle. Potholders similar to this one and the one pictured as Item 7.10 are readily available in the marketplace today.
Measurements: 4.5"L x 5"W
Price Range: $5-6

7.12 *Description:* Cabbage Rose Tablecloth
The tablecloth is a typical example of the type of floral tablecloths used extensively in American homes in the mid-20th century. The cabbage roses and butterflies on the tablecloth are bright and beautiful.
Measurements: 45.5"L x 50"W
Price Range: $20-25

7.13 Description: Zinnia Tablecloth
The very unusual and eye-catching example of a large round
tablecloth shown here is made of Belgian linen in the shape
of a zinnia. It came with a Leacock & Company, Inc. paper
label, also pictured here. The label has a photograph of this
same tablecloth in red.
Measurements: 70" diameter
Price Range: $35-40

7.14 Description: Daffodil Tablecloth
This burgundy and blue floral motif tablecloth is very striking. The geometric
design is not typical for printed floral tablecloths. A more traditional floral
tablecloth design is pictured as Item 7.12. There is minimal fading in some of
the blue areas.
Measurements: 51"L x 54"W
Price Range:
$35-40
$15-20 poor condition

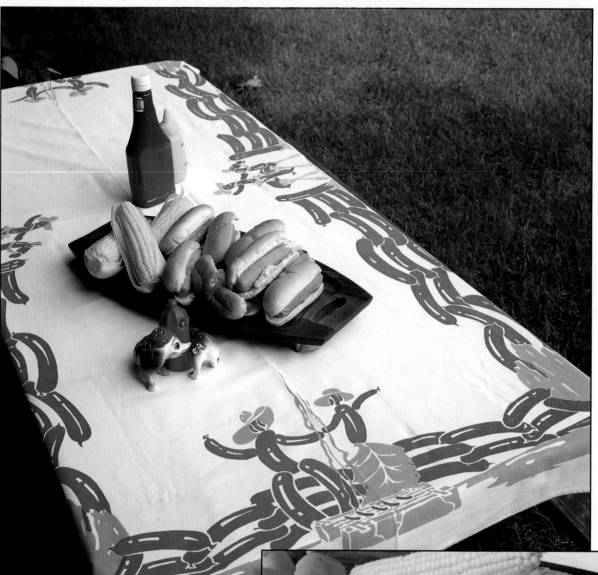

8.1 Description: Hot Dogs as Cowboys Tablecloth
Hot dogs have long been viewed as a typically all-American food. Sausages and wieners may have come from other countries but the hot dog, a sausage usually served on a long bun, is an American creation. *Reader's Digest America A to Z* suggests that the hot dog in a bun was the brainchild of a St. Louis sausage vendor sometime in the 1880s. The vendor, who was tired of giving his customers gloves to wear while eating their sausages, decided to serve his sausages on bread. This 19th century vendor could never have imagined the scene in this tablecloth. The "cowboys" are made from hot dogs and lettuce leaves. Two of the "cowboys" are astride hot dog "horses" with legs made from forks and spoons. Even the fences are made of hot dogs! We can't help but imagine "gobs" of mustard and ketchup squirting from their six-shooters in a gunfight. This is one of the most unique printed tablecloths with a barbecue theme that we have seen. It is the perfect size for a picnic table. Unfortunately, this particular example is in poor condition. It has numerous yellowish stains, holes, a few rips, and it is faded. We normally would not buy a piece in such terrible condition. However, this design is so wonderful we could not resist. In rare cases like this, we buy the piece to have the design in our collections with the intention of replacing it if we ever find an identical piece in better condition. The second photograph on this page is a close-up of the "cowboy" shown on each side of the tablecloth.
Measurements: 92"L x 36"W
Price Range:
$90-115
$10-15 poor condition

After the rationing of food and many other items during World War II ended, Americans breathed a collective sigh of relief. The postwar years were a time of economic expansion and abundance. An environment emerged that encouraged families to have children. Indeed, so many babies were born in the years after the war that a whole generation is now referred to as the baby boomers.

Growing families needed more room and many looked to the fast growing suburbs as the answer. As Americans migrated to the suburbs in droves after World War II, new lifestyles emerged that resulted in a trend toward more casual dining and entertaining. Americans took pleasure in flaunting their improved circumstances by entertaining friends and families in their new suburban homes. Eating outdoors quickly became fashionable for the new suburbanites and barbecues were all the rage. There are several interesting examples of barbecue motif tablecloths and towels in this chapter (Items 8.1 to 8.4).

Household linen designers quickly responded to the new passion for casual dining and entertaining. They experimented with bright, cheerful, humorous, and sometimes even bizarre designs to complement this new lifestyle. Their new designs quickly gained acceptance in the marketplace. Consequently, whimsical food and culinary themes on American household linen and handkerchiefs were plentiful during the "fun linen period."

Theme parties were also popular in the suburbs in the 1950s. An article by Jessamyn Neuhaus published in the *Journal of Social History* in spring 1999 and titled "The Way to a Man's Heart: Gender Roles, Domestic Ideology, and Cookbooks in the 1950s" discusses this trend as follows:

> On 1950s food the Sterns write: "to the suburban cook, food is never enough. Parties need themes; meals, accents." While everyday meals were, theoretically, simpler and easier to prepare, cookbooks encouraged women to throw "Hawaiian company dinners" or "country style" meals when "Everyone on the block is dressed for the hoe-down." The General Food's Kitchens Cookbook had complete menus for parties with themes such as "Come to the Mardi Gras," "Old South Open House," and "Alpine Fondue Party."

The "cowboy" hot dogs tablecloth (Item 8.1) was most likely made for use at suburban "country style hoe-downs."

As lifestyles changed, the expectations of American women likewise changed. Although most women were still content to remain in the home, a small but growing minority went to work outside the home. A book in *The Homemaker's Encyclopedia* series published in 1952 titled *Hostess's Complete Handbook* actually has a section giving advice to career women on how to find the time to plan parties.

As gender roles changed, men were expected to help around the house. Page 43 of the hostess handbook mentioned above addresses this shift in women's expectations as follows:

> Your husband's part in all this [entertaining] will usually consist in being a host after the guests arrive. Mixing and serving the drinks if you have them, carving, and some of the serving will be part of his share. ...The part of a good host is, in itself, a very important and helpful one, but, nowadays, there are many men able and very willing to do more. For example, it is the rule, rather than the exception, for the host to be responsible for the cooking on charcoal grills, barbecues, or any outdoor fire. If your husband, like so many modern men, is something of an amateur chef, you might plan an occasional party menu around one of his specialties.

The Neuhaus article mentioned earlier described women's reaction to men in the kitchen as follows:

> To assuage any fears that Dad might be really serious about moving into the kitchen, he was encouraged to wear large aprons with macho slogans, which were the opposite of her frilly ones and wild oversize utensils, which were clearly inappropriate for the kitchen.

A classic example of this type of "macho" apron is pictured as Item 13.3 in Chapter 13.

We have included several examples of household linen both in this chapter and elsewhere in the book that depict men and women engaged in various household tasks as they adapted to their new roles in the 20th century. The printed towel with the gentleman in the kitchen learning how to cook is a perfect example (Item 8.18). It is also interesting to note the mother's face on the printed towel pictured as Item 8.33. She appears to be showing the frustration with her role as a housewife that women began to express more openly in this period.

After the initial postwar euphoria had worn off, Americans once again began to worry about their weight. Although counting calories had first found its way into the national consciousness in the early 1900s, it reached new heights in the second half of the 20th century. The saying "a person can never be too rich or too thin" was very popular. Enterprises catering to this growing national obsession with weight eventually "sprang up" across America. In 1948 Esther Manz founded TOPS (Take Off Pounds Sensibly), which was by some accounts the first support group for weight loss. By 1960, Jack La Lanne's exercise show was one of the most popular daily television shows in the country. And in 1963 Jean Nidetch founded Weight Watchers.

8.2 Description: Rare, Medium, Well Towel, Tammis Keefe
A wonderful barbecue theme towel designed by Tammis Keefe is seen here. "Warranted All Linen" is printed on the original paper label, which is attached. This towel was also made with a gray background. It is difficult to find this towel in either color. The brown version pictured is the more collectible towel.
Measurements: 30"L x 16"W
Price Range: $45-50 either color

Textile designers quickly joined the slim and fit bandwagon, and in the 1950s they began to design textiles that appealed to a calorie counting, exercise conscious American public. They designed a large array of printed handkerchiefs, napkins, towels, and tablecloths with pictures of various foods and their calorie counts (Items 8.5 to 8.8). They also designed both printed and embroidered towels and handkerchiefs with people exercising (Items 8.10 to 8.12).

Anthropomorphism is prevalent in this chapter as in others. The combination of food and anthropomorphic themes resulted in some outstanding fun household linen designs in the mid-20th century. Illustrations of food and kitchen utensils exhibiting human characteristics in this chapter include: the towel depicting a fish dressed as a chef (Item 8.21); the dish towel with marching pots and pans (Item 8.36); and the hot dog "cowboys" tablecloth seen on the opposite page.

Among the various design themes discussed in this chapter, anthropomorphic and barbecue theme household linen is the most prized by today's collectors. Tablecloths and towels with these themes command the highest prices. Signed examples such as the Tammis Keefe tablecloth (Item 8.4), the Fabrés chef tablecloth (Item 8.35), and the Vera towels (Items 8.22 and 8.23) are also very desirable.

8.3 Description: Barbecue Recipe Handkerchief
This handkerchief helpfully lists the standard barbecue menu: hamburger, steak, franks, bread and butter, dill pickles, and watermelon. It still has its original Franshaw paper label as well as the original 38 cent price tag from The Higbee Co. The scalloped edge is machine embroidered.
Measurements: 13"L x 13.875"W
Price Range: $25-28

8.4 Description: Barbecue Tablecloth, Tammis Keefe
This cheerful tablecloth signed by Tammis Keefe has all the implements and ingredients needed for a barbecue. It is one of the most interesting Tammis Keefe tablecloth patterns we have seen. This particular example shows some signs of wear. There are also some very faint stains and the red checked area is faded in spots. This design was made in at least one other color version with the checked area in gray.
Measurements: 84"L x 53.5"W
Price Range:
$90-125
$50-55 poor condition

8.5 Description: Calories Tablecloth with Napkins
This type of tablecloth and napkins set was popular in the 1950s. The tablecloth still has the original tag. The 1952 copyright date is on the tag, the tablecloth, and the six napkins. Hedaya Brothers produced the set. They also made a matching towel. There is little doubt that this set was designed to provide American families with an entertaining way of counting calories.
Measurements:
52" square, tablecloth
15.5"L x 15"W, napkins
Price Range: $45-65 seven-piece set

8.6 Description: Calories Towel
A bikini clad lady surrounded by various foods and their calorie counts is standing on a scale in the middle of this towel. She should have remembered to remove her shoes for the best possible result.
Measurements: 28"L x 16.5"W
Price Range: $25-30

8.7 *Description:* Calories Handkerchiefs
Burmel made these two very similar cotton handkerchiefs. Some of the foods on the two handkerchiefs are identical while others are not. These handkerchiefs are easy to find and they are perennial favorites with collectors.
Measurements: 13.5" square, each handkerchief
Price Range: $12-15 each handkerchief

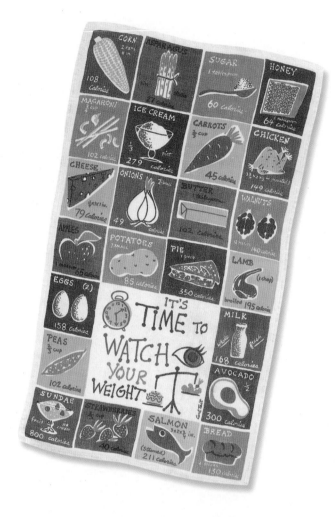

8.8 *Description:* It's Time to Watch Your Weight Towel, Carl Tait
Carl Tait signed this amusing calories towel. Note the strange method of measuring helpings of salmon, chicken, and cheese. Who would have guessed that you needed to measure food portions in inches? As with all Carl Tait towels, this one is difficult to find.
Measurements: 29"L x 16"W
Price Range: $30-35

8.9 *Description:* Pinup Beauty on a Scale With Her Admiring Poodles Towel
The pinup lady on the guest towel is weighing herself while one of her admiring puppies is adding to her weight with its paw. Naughty dog!
Measurements: 18"L x 11.5"W
Price Range: $25-28

8.10 *Description:* Breakfast and Lunch Towels, Pat Prichard
Low calorie breakfast and lunch menus for each day of the week are listed on these linen towels. Both towels are signed Pat Prichard. The breakfast towel has the number 56 beside the signature and the lunch towel has the number 51. Pat Prichard also designed a towel with dinner menus as part of this series. (It is not pictured here.) Very trim young ladies, engaged in calisthenics, are interspersed among the menus. At the bottom of both towels seen here there are well-dressed gentlemen holding flowers and jewelry and admiring the women. The recipe for success according to these towels is: Eat the correct foods and exercise to maintain your figure so you can attract a man to shower you with gifts and keep you in the style to which you could very quickly become accustomed! All three towels were also made with at least two other color backgrounds, pink and dark brown.
Measurements: 29"L x 16.375"W
Price Range: $30-35 each towel

8.11 *Description:* Bikini Clad Ladies Exercising
A set of four hand-embroidered towels with scantily clad ladies doing various exercises is pictured here. The bikinis are appliqué. Each of the exercises is designed to firm up a specific part of the body. The Torso Trimmer and The Fanny Shaver sound like medieval torture devices. The things we do in the name of vanity!
Measurements: 19.5"L x 12"W, each towel
Price Range: $20-22 each towel

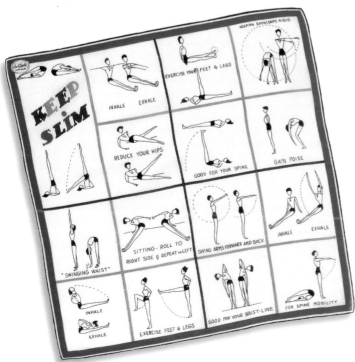

8.12 *Description:* Keep Slim Handkerchief
This handkerchief has its original Carol Stanley paper label. It has fifteen squares with different exercises to keep slim represented in each square. If you follow the advice in the squares, you will gain poise, keep your good waistline, reduce your hips, keep your spine mobile, and improve your feet and legs. Clearly, almost everyone could use this handkerchief!
Measurements: 13"L x 13.25"W
Price Range: $15-18

8.13 *Description:* Dieter's Lying Towel
There is an abundance of crying towels on the market; however, there are very few lying towels. Most readers will be able to relate to one or more of these excuses. We sure do!
Measurements: 27"L x 16"W
Price Range: $20-22

8.14 *Description:* Sweet 'N Low Advertisement Towel
This towel is an advertisement for Sweet 'N Low. The calorie equivalencies for Sweet 'N Low versus sugar are given at the top. Calorie counts for various popular foods are also listed on the towel. Ben and Marvin Eisenstadt introduced Sweet 'N Low in the United States in 1957. This product is still sweetening the planet from its base in Brooklyn, New York.
Measurements: 27.5"L x 16"W
Price Range: $25-28

8.15 *Description:* Market-to-Market Towel
The tag on the towel reads "Home Beautiful Linens by Vickie." An additional tag says it was made in Japan. This towel takes us back to a time when crabs were $1.46 a dozen and fish was 49¢ per pound. Those were the good old days!
Measurements: 29"L x 15.75"W
Price Range: $15-20

8.16 *Description:* Crocheted Corn Potholder
Similar homemade potholders were very popular in the mid-20th century. Almost every household during that time period had a few crocheted potholders in the kitchen. However, most of the potholders were square or round rather than figural in shape. This potholder is collectible because of its good quality crochet and interesting shape.
Measurements: 7"L x 5.75"W
Price Range: $8-12

8.17 *Description:* Lobster Dinner Handkerchief, Tammis Keefe
This very striking example of a handkerchief with food as the subject matter has Tammis Keefe's signature in the lower left-hand corner. The handkerchief is showing a fully set table with a bright red lobster on a platter in the center. This design is very popular among Tammis Keefe collectors. This handkerchief was also made with a blue background; however, the red version pictured here is more common.
Measurements: 15.25"L x 14.75"W
Price Range: $30-35 either color

8.18 *Description:* The Master in the Kitchen Towel
This towel shows the changing role of men in postwar America. This particular male cook appears to be on the low end of the learning curve. While he ponders his recipe book, the pots on the stove are boiling over and the dog is enjoying the food spilling out of the pot onto his lap.
Measurements: 25.5"L x 16.75"W
Price Range: $18-28

8.19 *Description:* Casserole and Coffeepot Tablecloth
The coffee pot, casserole dish, condiment set, salt and pepper shakers, wine bottle, and glass are representative of 1950s designs. This tablecloth is perfect for a 1950s theme party, especially when the same or similar serving pieces are used to complement it.
Measurements: 54"L x 46"W
Price Range: $20-25

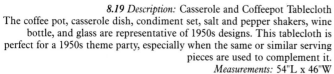

8.20 *Description:* Miro Style Tablecloth
This ecru tablecloth resembles a Miro painting. If the host or hostess follows the menu suggestions on the tablecloth, the event will be a gastronomical success. The menu suggestions include wine, cheese, grilled hot dogs, fish, chicken, clams, fruits, tomatoes, and other vegetables. The ducks on two corners of the tablecloth and the picnic basket suggest a party or picnic beside the water.
Measurements: 72"L x 53.5 "W
Price Range: $50-75

8.21 *Description:* Betty Boop's Exploding Pot Towel, and Fish Cooking the Chef Towel
There is a Betty Boop-like quality to the wide-eyed female cook on the top towel. She is shocked to find her culinary masterpiece boiling over the edge of the pot. She has thrown her hands up in dismay. The chef on the bottom towel seems to be at the wrong end of the pan. The smiling fish in chef's regalia is taking great delight in frying the chef. Both towels are hand embroidered and color has been added to highlight the lady, fish, chef, pot, and pan. Each of the towels has its design on one end only.
Measurements:
27.25"L x 17.25"W, Betty Boop towel
27"L x 17.5"W, fish towel
Price Range: $25-35 each towel

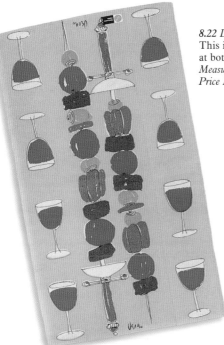

8.22 Description: Shish-kabob Towel, Vera
This is a perfect towel for a summer barbecue. It has Vera's signature without the ladybug at both ends. Its original paper label reads "Vera Kitchen Fashion Originals, All Linen."
Measurements: 28.5"L x 15.75"W
Price Range: $35-40

8.23 Description: Lobster Towel, Vera
This towel shows all the necessary ingredients for a wonderful seafood dinner. The colors are bright and fun. The design is by Vera.
Measurements: 29"L x 16.5"W
Price Range: $35-40

8.24 Description: Christmas Placemats, Vera
There are eight Vera placemats in this original gift box. The cover of the box reads "A Holiday Dinner, painted for your visual and gastronomic enjoyment, this December 25th, 1960." The advertisement, which accompanied the box, says the placemats are called "Veramats, the new convertible place mats that can be folded and used as giant lap-size napkins." The ad goes on to say that when a placemat is not a placemat "it's a witty and wonderful Veramat." The placemats feature recipes for baked fish, mince pie, vegetable soup, and holiday ham casserole. Each placemat has the Vera logo and ladybug.
Measurements: 18.5"L x 12"W
Price Range: $45-65

8.25 *Description:* Cross-Stitch Chef Tablecloth With Napkins

This hand-embroidered tablecloth depicts chefs carrying baskets of vegetables and sharpening their carving knives. These rotund chefs certainly appear to be enjoying their own cooking. There are four matching napkins as seen on the tablecloth. Each of the napkins has one of the chefs' faces embroidered on one corner.

Measurements:
10.5"L x 12"W, each napkin
53.5"L x 35"W, tablecloth
Price Range: $40-45 five-piece set

8.27 *Description:* Rabbit Stew Towel, C.P. Meier

This is a tongue-in-cheek recipe towel with instructions to first catch the rabbit before you can begin the stew. Signed by C.P. Meier. This towel was also made in yellow.

Measurements: 28"L x 15.5"W
Price Range: $22-28 either color

8.26 *Description:* Poodle Chef Towels

Poodles in cute aprons and chef's hats bring their charm to the kitchen. The poodle to the left is preparing breakfast pancakes. Many of the needed ingredients for the pancakes are on the border of the towel. However, the poodle may be somewhat confused by the cocktail glass and wine bottle also included on the border. Oh well, maybe the pancakes are for brunch. The poodle chef to the right is engaged in making soup or stew. Some of the needed vegetables are sitting on the edge of the towel waiting to be included in this culinary masterpiece. The original label on the towel to the left reads "Parisian Prints, All Pure Linen."

Measurements:
28.25"L x 16.25"W, Parisian Print
27.5"L x 15.5"W
Price Range: $25-35 each towel

8.28 Description: Food Handkerchief, Pat Prichard
Pat Prichard designed this amusing handkerchief depicting various types of food. She also made another very similar handkerchief with various types of seafood rather than meat. She used similar whimsical food motifs in an illustration she did for a 1957 magazine ad for cruises on Italian Lines "Sunny Southern Route."
Measurements: 15" square
Price Range: $12-15

8.29 Description: What's Cooking Towels, Lois Long
Breakfast is the subject matter for the Lois Long towel to the left. At the time this towel was made, eggs were considered to be healthy for one and all. It is interesting to note how suggestions for healthy eating have changed over the years. The second towel in the photograph features cooking corn. Both towels have labels sewn into the hem on one end that read "Original Town House."
Measurements:
27.5"L x 16.25"W, breakfast towel
29"L x 15.25"W, corn towel
Price Range: $25-30 each towel

8.30 Description: Appliquéd Salt and Pepper Shakers Kitchen Towel
The appliquéd salt and pepper shakers on this towel have embroidered birds perched on them. There is also embroidered fruit on the towel. This scene projects the feeling of fun in the kitchen.
Measurements: 23"L x 17"W
Price Range: $10-15

8.31 *Description:* Little Boy Washing Dishes Towel
This towel takes us back to the days when dishwashers were not common in the kitchen. The sulky little boy wearing an apron is washing dishes as his pals taunt him through the window. The footballs, football helmets, and megaphones on the side of the towel give the observer reason to believe the little boy's mind is not on the dishes. It appears he has been grounded. A towel with this subject matter would not have been popular earlier in the century. The likely subject matter for an earlier towel would be a little girl with a smiling face doing the dishes. This towel is an interesting example of household linen portraying the changing role of the male in American society.
Measurements: 28.5"L x 16"W
Price Range: $25-30

8.32 Description: Policeman Kitchen Towel, Tom Lamb
Tom Lamb, a noted designer of children's handkerchiefs, designed this cartoon-like towel with a scene of a policeman helping himself to a fresh pie. The scene is printed on only one end of the towel. Towels by Tom Lamb are difficult to find.
Measurements: 26.5"L x 17"W
Price Range: $25-30

Two Versions of Mom in the Kitchen in Mid-20th Century America

8.33 Description: Home Sweet Home Kitchen Towel
Earlier in the century, Home Sweet Home scenes were very idealized. Mom would be smiling, the children would be well dressed and well behaved, and all would be peaceful. By the middle of the century, reality had started to creep into these types of scenes. This towel shows the essential elements of Home Sweet Home in mid-20th century America. Mom is in the kitchen, the children are playing, and the household includes a dog and a cat. However, instead of smiling as she would have been on towels made earlier in the century, mom is clutching her head and looking very distressed. We all know what it feels like to be trying to do too many things at the same time.
Measurements: 26.5"L x 15.25"W
Price Range: $25-30

8.34 Description: Dad Kissing Mom Kitchen Towel
Dad in his work clothes (a business suit) sneaks a kiss in the kitchen while the Scottish Terrier watches. The children and the cat are in the background playing. All is well in mid-20th century America.
Measurements: 28.5"L x 14.5"W
Price Range: $40-50

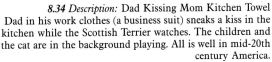

8.35 Description: French Chef Tablecloth, Fabrés
According to this humorous linen tablecloth, the four main food groups are beef, chicken, pork, and seafood. The tablecloth brings a whole new meaning to the term "playing with your food" as one chef toasts a bull decked out in a top hat and red checked jacket while another chef prepares to take a bow with a wine tasting pig. The quality of the printing could have been better. Traces of the red ink are scattered around some of the figures such as the rooster and the crab; however, the design is wonderful. The tablecloth is signed Fabrés and still retains its Leacock & Company, Inc. paper label. The label reads "Leacock Quality Hand Prints, Linen, 5 Pc bridge set, Gourmet." The matching napkins are missing. Leacock & Company, Inc. also made a matching towel, which is not pictured here. Both the tablecloth and the towel are difficult to find.
Measurements: 35.5"L x 35"W
Price Range:
$75-85 tablecloth
$40-45 towel

8.36 *Description:* Kitchen Parade Towel
This pattern depicting marching dishes and eating utensils is aptly titled "Kitchen Parade." It is a Wonder-Dri towel by Startex. The towel has numerous yellow stains. Startex made a similar towel in red and white with smiling dancing pots and pans as the subject matter. The writing on the edge of the second towel says "If you keep this jumbo towel handy your pots and pans will shine just dandy." Both towels are very popular among collectors. An American company, the Red and White Kitchen Company, is currently reproducing the "Kitchen Parade" pattern in dishtowels and potholders. The new dishtowels can be differentiated from the vintage examples in several ways: the new towels are 30" square and come with a tag sewn into one hem stating that they are made with 100% Egyptian cotton. The new towels retail for $12. To the best of our knowledge, vintage potholders with this design were never made.
Measurements: 30.25"L x 27.25"W
Price Range:
$35-40 each towel, vintage
$5-10 each towel, poor condition, vintage

8.37 *Description:* Elizabeth and Spoon, Appliquéd Kitchen Towel
Elizabeth is in the kitchen with her high heels and her darling appliquéd apron. She appears to be having a discussion with her cooking spoon. If the spoon could talk, we think it would have some interesting tales. Was Elizabeth ready to shed her apron for a career as a Wall Street banker?
Measurements: 29"L x 28.25 "W
Price Range: $10-12

8.38 *Description:* Recipe Apron
Numerous recipes including a recipe for apple pie, the all-American desert, are shown on the apron. A recipe for that most difficult of dishes, a fresh green salad, is also included. This apron is shown with a Dinah Shore cookbook titled *Someone's in the Kitchen with Dinah.*
Measurements: 19"L x 19"W gathered at the waist
Price Range: $10-12

8.39 Description: Appliquéd Strawberry Cocktail Napkins
This set of six hand-appliquéd linen cocktail napkins is a good example of the fine workmanship and beautiful design that characterize a great deal of the high-end household linen produced in Madeira in the 20th century. Although not visible in the photograph, the napkins still have their original paper label that reads "Madeira Superbia L.D.A., Trademark Pride of Madeira, Fabrica Rua Do Carmo, 27-1., Funchal, Madeira."
Measurements: 6"L x 7.75"W
Price Range: $60-75 set of six

8.40 Description: Embroidered Fish Shaped Napkin Rings
The six fish-shaped linen napkin rings are hand embroidered. Four are embroidered with brown cotton thread and two with blue. Figural linen napkins rings are extremely difficult to find. They are a great conversation piece for dinner parties or luncheons. When we show these pieces to people, most of them do not know what they are because they are so uncommon. People usually assume they were meant to be decorative pieces of appliqué to add to towels or placemats. They are in unused condition, still stitched together, and have their original metal manufacturer's tags. It is likely they were made in Madeira.
Measurements: 9.125"L x 2.5" deep at the widest point
Price Range: $3-4 each

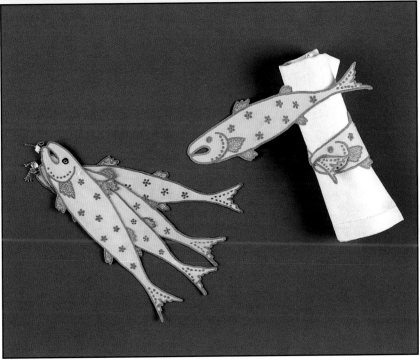

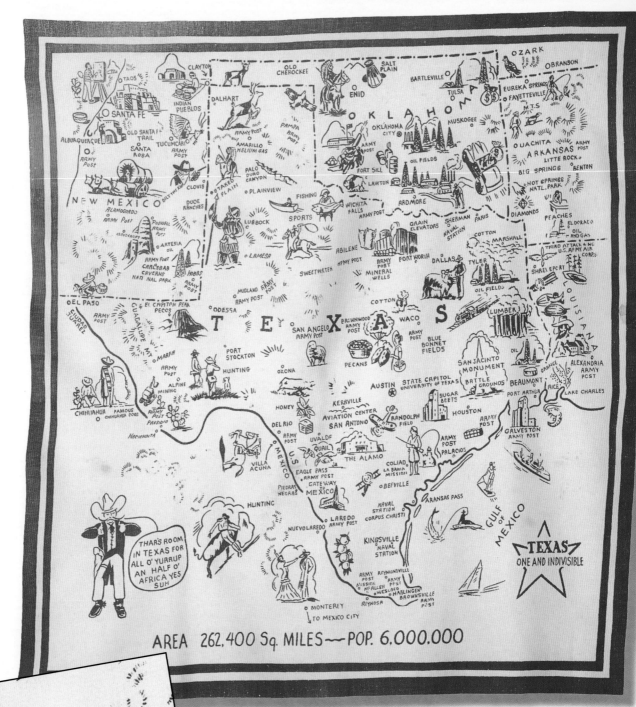

9.1 Description: Texas Tablecloth

This tablecloth shows Texas, the Lone Star State, and various neighboring states. The Texas star with the words "One and Indivisible" appears on the bottom right-hand side. There are also scenes of oil fields, cities, the Alamo, military facilities, and various whimsical graphics commonly associated with Texas on the tablecloth. "Pop. 6,000,000" is printed on the bottom left-hand side. Since the population of Texas was 7.7 million in 1950, it is likely that the tablecloth was produced in the 1940s. The second photo is a close-up of one of the whimsical graphics. It shows a Texas cowboy letting us know "Thar's room in Texas for all o' yurrup and half o' Africa yes suh." The cowboy makes this cloth unusual. Tablecloths with states as the subject matter are usually more conservative.

Measurements: 51"L x 47"W
Price Range: $75-100

Chapter 9
Geography and Travel

In the late 1940s and early 1950s Americans in ever increasing numbers began to travel for business and pleasure. The idea of a yearly family vacation became part of the American family dream. This was facilitated by the interstate highways built after World War II, which were forays into tourism; and by air conditioning, which made travel to the south and southwest more feasible during the summer months. The most popular travel destinations for the middle class were within the United States. Europe remained a popular travel destination for the upper class. It was a status symbol to travel and travelers found great pleasure in returning home with souvenirs of their excursions for themselves, their family, and friends. Textiles were often purchased as souvenirs and many of these souvenirs are very popular collectibles today. Souvenir towels, tablecloths, napkins, and handkerchiefs were very popular gifts.

The concept of printing maps on textiles actually predates the 20th century—in the 18th century people used information printed on textiles to help them find their way on trips. Maps of American states were among the most popular textile souvenirs of the postwar period. California, Florida, and New York were among the most popular travel destinations during the "fun linen period." There are many examples of maps of these states on handkerchiefs, napkins, towels, and tablecloths produced during this period. Maps were also printed on aprons; however, they were not very popular and examples of state map aprons from this period are scarce. Scenes of the most popular tourist attractions in a state were usually depicted on the maps. Sometimes these scenes were quite amusing. One of our favorite state maps is pictured on the adjoining page. This map of Texas features a Texas cowboy comparing the size of Texas to Europe.

Maps of city scenes were also popular subject matter. There are many examples of American and European cities and city scenes in this chapter. New York and Paris scenes were particular favorites for the textile designers. As we turn our attention to cities, we discover that animals recur as popular subject matter and poodles are featured here as they are in many other chapters. The designers could not resist the fantasy of animals enjoying travel in New York and Europe. The poodle towels (Item 9.18) are an excellent example of the blend of anthropomorphism and travel, which were both popular "fun linen period" themes.

Household linen and handkerchiefs were also produced to commemorate famous events. Commemorative pieces are collectible and often difficult to find. For example, tablecloths, towels, and handkerchiefs featuring maps and pavilions from various World's Fairs were produced. We have included a tablecloth (Item 9.22) and a handkerchief (Item 9.23) from the 1939 World's Fair in this chapter.

The 1939 World's Fair in New York was particularly important to Americans because the country was emerging from the Depression and the fair helped Americans feel revitalized. Tens of thousands of them visited the fair each day. The fair was called "The World of Tomorrow" and there were displays featuring televisions, electric washers and dryers, and refrigerators capable of making their own ice. The General Motors "Futurama" exhibit featured a vision of America in 1960 with people living in collapsible houses and driving cars powered by "liquid air." Visitors to the GM Pavilion were given a button saying "I have seen the future" as they exited the pavilion.

Some of the souvenirs related to travel were signed by famous designers. The designer items were generally more distinctive and creative than the typical travel souvenirs. Tammis Keefe, Tony Sarg, Carl Tait, Pat Prichard, and Vera designed some of the items we have included in this chapter. In general, souvenir handkerchiefs and tablecloths are the most collectible items relating to geography.

9.2 Description: Las Vegas Tablecloth.
This mint unused tablecloth displays scenes of Las Vegas and some of its most famous casinos. The New Frontier, one of the casino hotels on the tablecloth, helped us to date it. This casino hotel was called the New Frontier from 1955 to 1967, which leads us to believe the tablecloth was made within that time period. This casino hotel was renamed the Frontier in 1967, and renamed New Frontier again in 1992. "A Sahuaro Brand Table Cloth, Hand Printed, Color Fast, Superior Hand-Prints, Los Angeles 13, Calif." is printed on the label attached to the tablecloth with glue. There is a crap table in the center of the tablecloth and horseshoes in each corner. Each of the horseshoes has a scene of Las Vegas in its center.
Measurements: 54" square
Price Range: $100-125

9.3 Description: Florida Tablecloth
Well-known tourist spots throughout Florida are listed on this tablecloth. Orlando is included on the tablecloth and it mentions the Singing Tower as the main attraction and not Walt Disney World, which opened in 1971. Cape Canaveral, the principal launching site for United States earth orbiting satellites and manned space flight since 1947, is also not mentioned; therefore, we believe this tablecloth was made before 1947. Although the colors have not faded, there are numerous yellowish stains, which may be difficult to remove.
Measurements: 50"L x 53"W
Price Range:
$40-45
$10-15 poor condition

9.4 Description: Two Delaware Handkerchiefs, Tammis Keefe
This linen handkerchief shown in two color combinations depicts famous places in Wilmington, Delaware. It is signed Tammis Keefe. Ms. Keefe made a number of handkerchiefs depicting famous places or cities in the United States. Her handkerchiefs featuring places and cities from New York and California usually command the highest prices.
Measurements: 13"L x 13.75"W each color
Price Range: $10-12 each

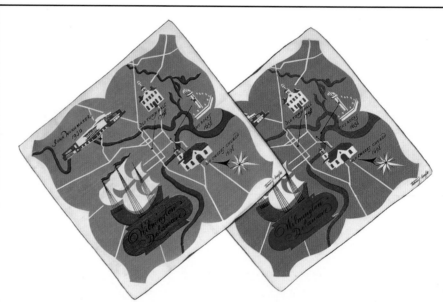

9.5 Description: California Apron
This apron shows the state of California with many of its sights and cities. This piece has excellent graphics including: a bathing beauty in Palm Springs, a bear in Sequoia National Park, Hollywood Movie Studios, and Fisherman's Wharf to name a few. It is very difficult to find aprons with scenes of states.
Measurements: 20.5"L x 16.5" gathered at the waist
Price Range: $30-35

9.6 *Description:* States Cocktail Napkins
Seven linen cocktail napkins with maps of various American states are pictured here. The napkins come in four different colors: pink, blue, green, and yellow. Not pictured is an eighth napkin depicting Pennsylvania. It is possible that napkins for all the other states were also made. However, to date, we have only seen the eight states mentioned.
Measurements: 5"L x 7"W
Price Range: $25-30 set of eight

9.7 *Description:* New Orleans Tablecloth
The musicians and the scenes of New Orleans are beautifully illustrated on this tablecloth. The Mississippi Ferry Boat, the Mardi Gras, the French Quarter and many other scenes of the city are depicted on the edges of the tablecloth. Two corners of the tablecloth have musicians playing New Orleans jazz. This tablecloth was also made with a red background. It was produced by Parisian Prints.
Measurements: 53.5"L x 48.5"W
Price Range: $125-150 either color

9.8 *Description:* New York City Handkerchiefs, Carl Tait
The two linen handkerchiefs are signed Carl Tait. The first handkerchief depicts various famous New York City scenes such as the Statue of Liberty and Times Square. The second shows people in a double-decker bus in New York City. A third New York handkerchief (not shown) depicts a scene from Central Park. Carl Tait also designed handkerchiefs for various other cities and states in the United States. To date, the most expensive handkerchief in the city and state series is one of the two Chicago handkerchiefs. The "Chicago That Wonderful Town" handkerchief sold for a record $180.50 at auction in August 2001. In terms of rarity, the "New York Central Park" and "Chicago That Wonderful Town" are the most difficult to find. The Herrmann Handkerchief Company produced these handkerchiefs. Our readers should note that we believe the price realized for "Chicago That Wonderful Town" was inflated and a fair market price range for the handkerchief is indicated below.
Measurements:
14.5"L x 14.625"W, each handkerchief
Price Range:
$20-25 Cincinnati, Dayton, and Harrisburg
$25-30 Boston, Chicago (various city scenes), Cleveland, Florida, and St. Louis
$30-35 two New York pictured here
$40-45 Connecticut, Los Angeles, San Francisco, and Seattle
$45-55 New York Central Park
$55-85 Chicago That Wonderful Town

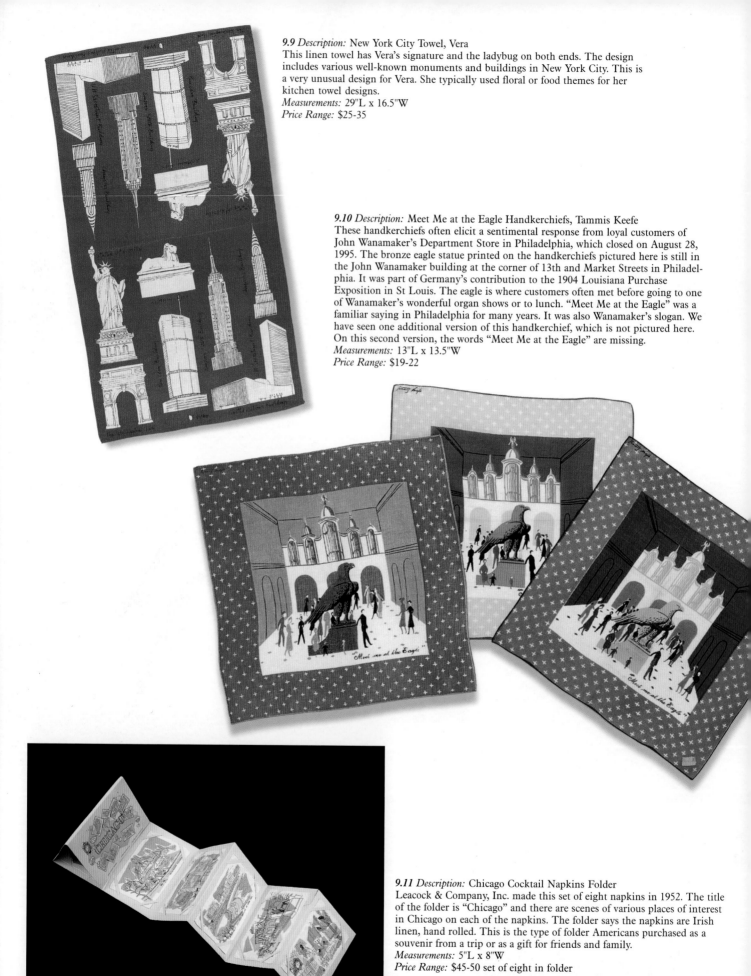

9.9 *Description:* New York City Towel, Vera
This linen towel has Vera's signature and the ladybug on both ends. The design includes various well-known monuments and buildings in New York City. This is a very unusual design for Vera. She typically used floral or food themes for her kitchen towel designs.
Measurements: 29"L x 16.5"W
Price Range: $25-35

9.10 *Description:* Meet Me at the Eagle Handkerchiefs, Tammis Keefe
These handkerchiefs often elicit a sentimental response from loyal customers of John Wanamaker's Department Store in Philadelphia, which closed on August 28, 1995. The bronze eagle statue printed on the handkerchiefs pictured here is still in the John Wanamaker building at the corner of 13th and Market Streets in Philadelphia. It was part of Germany's contribution to the 1904 Louisiana Purchase Exposition in St Louis. The eagle is where customers often met before going to one of Wanamaker's wonderful organ shows or to lunch. "Meet Me at the Eagle" was a familiar saying in Philadelphia for many years. It was also Wanamaker's slogan. We have seen one additional version of this handkerchief, which is not pictured here. On this second version, the words "Meet Me at the Eagle" are missing.
Measurements: 13"L x 13.5"W
Price Range: $19-22

9.11 *Description:* Chicago Cocktail Napkins Folder
Leacock & Company, Inc. made this set of eight napkins in 1952. The title of the folder is "Chicago" and there are scenes of various places of interest in Chicago on each of the napkins. The folder says the napkins are Irish linen, hand rolled. This is the type of folder Americans purchased as a souvenir from a trip or as a gift for friends and family.
Measurements: 5"L x 8"W
Price Range: $45-50 set of eight in folder

9.12 *Description:* New Orleans Towel, Pat Prichard
Creole cooking, riverboats, and jazz bring New Orleans to mind. This towel is signed Pat Prichard. She also designed several other towels using this same layout and incorporating well-known items from various other American cities or regions such as New England.
Measurements: 29"L x 15"W
Price Range: $22-25

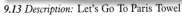

9.13 *Description:* Let's Go To Paris Towel
Paris has always been a very popular tourist destination. In this scene we see an artist selling his paintings in one of the open-air markets of Paris. A well-dressed lady accompanied by her poodle is admiring the art. This pure linen towel was made in Ireland.
Measurements: 32"L x 21"W
Price Range: $15-20

9.14 *Description:* Children's Handkerchief, Norway
This children's handkerchief shows a map of Norway with the sun smiling down on it. Flowers, the sun, a ship and other things associated with the country are nicely illustrated on the handkerchief. The children are very cute.
Measurements: 8.75" square
Price Range: $8-10

9.15 *Description:* Foreign Currencies Handkerchief, Tammis Keefe
Tammis Keefe signed this linen handkerchief, which still has its original J.H. Kimball & Company, Inc. paper label. The handkerchief actually gives currency conversions for the United States dollar versus the British pound, the Italian lira, the French franc, and the Spanish peseta. One thousand Italian lira equaled $1.69 in the United States when this handkerchief was made. How times have changed. This same amount of lira is currently worth less than $0.50.
Measurements: 15" square
Price Range: $28-30

9.16 *Description:* Venice Towel, Pat Prichard
This towel incorporates various scenes of Venice. It is signed Pat Prichard and the copyright year is 1955. "Original Town House, Kitchen Decoratives, Pure Linen, Fast Color Guaranteed" is printed on the label which is sewn into the hem on one end of the towel.
Measurements: 29"L x 16"W
Price Range: $40-45

9.17 *Description:* Park Avenue Poodles Guest Towels
The three poodles sitting beside signs on Park Avenue are looking longingly at the print of the poodles in Paris. All three seem ready for a Paris vacation. The towel to the left and the towel in the middle are embroidered and printed. The towel to the right is printed. All three of the dogs have a beaded eye and the dog to the right has a beaded collar. A towel in our collections, identical to the left and middle towels pictured here, has its original paper label. The label reads "Pure Linen, Bucilla, Reg. U.S. Pat. Off., Hand Thread Drawn." These towels are popular collectibles.
Measurements: 19.5"L x 11.25"W
Price Range: $20-28

9.18 Description: Poodles in London and Paris Guest Towels
Poodles were on the move in the 1950s! Some of their favorite travel destinations were London and Paris. The male poodle in this scene is very appropriately dressed in his tuxedo, top hat, and cane as he travels to Rome, London, and Paris. The fashionably dressed female poodle is window-shopping at Christian Dore, presumably in Paris. Both poodles have partially embroidered bodies.
Measurements: 17.75"L x 14.75"W
Price Range: $35-40 each

9.19 Description: Bon Voyage Handkerchief, Carl Tait
This handkerchief still has its original Herrmann Handkerchief Company paper label, which states it was made from Irish linen with a hand rolled hem. Carl Tait used this type of lettering in many of his designs. He designed at least one other Bon Voyage handkerchief as well as several other handkerchiefs for special occasions including one for birthdays and one for Valentine's Day. He also designed at least one Thank You handkerchief.
Measurements: 15.125" square
Price Range: $40-45

9.20 *Description:* Europe Tablecloth
This cotton tablecloth shows scenes of European cities and cities bordering the Mediterranean. It is a perfect gift for the world traveler on your shopping list. The edge of the tablecloth has emblems of some of the countries pictured on the tablecloth.
Measurements: 59"L x 51"W
Price Range: $45-55

9.21 Description: Leaning Tower of Pisa Towel, Pat Prichard
The copyright date on this linen towel signed Pat Prichard is 1955. "Original Town House Kitchen Decoratives, Pure Linen, Fast Color Guaranteed" is printed on the label sewn in the hem. The towel comes in at least two different color combinations. In addition to the version pictured here, we have also seen this towel with the tower in green against a rust background.
Measurements: 29"L x 16"W
Price Range: $28-30

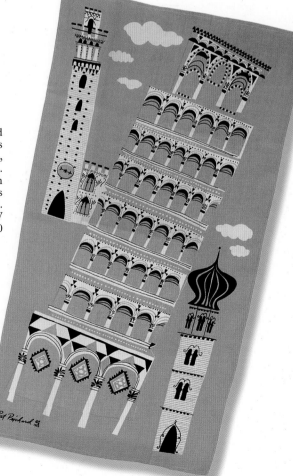

9.22 Description: 1939 World's Fair Tablecloth, Tony Sarg
The tablecloth shows scenes from the 1939 World's Fair in New York City. It was designed and signed by Tony Sarg. The circle in the center is a map of the fair and the borders depict various pavilions from the fair. Fifty-eight foreign countries and thirty-eight states had exhibits at the fair. Mr. Sarg designed numerous items for the fair including a paper map of the fairgrounds.
Measurements: 45"L x 43"W
Price Range: $175-195

9.23 Description: 1939 World's Fair Handkerchief
This handkerchief is in mint condition with its original paper label on the back, which states it is made of linen. It lists major events in New York's history starting in 1609 with the exploration of the Hudson River. Textile souvenir items in mint condition from the 1939 World's Fair held in New York City are difficult to find. Most of the items we have seen show significant wear, holes, or stains.
Collection of: Lisa Heller
Measurements: 12.75"L x 13"W
Price Range: $25-30

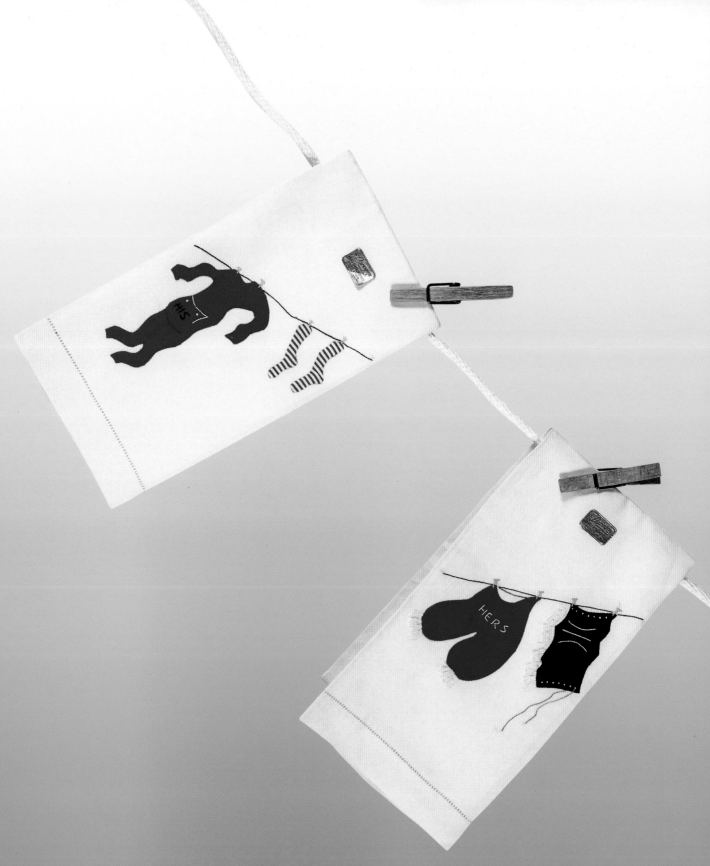

10.1 *Description:* Appliquéd His and Hers Clothes on a Clothesline Towels
The pair of linen appliquéd towels pictured above still has the original paper labels
that read "Paragon Needlecraft, Hand Embroidered Pure Linen, Cotton Decoration." His towel has a man's long johns and socks while Her towel has a woman's
lace trimmed bloomers and corset. This particular design is very popular with
collectors of his and hers household linen.
Measurements: 19.5"L x 12.875"W, each towel
Price Range: $40-45 pair

Chapter 10
His and Hers

His and hers household linen was produced throughout most of the 20th century. The height of its popularity was during the mid-20th century. The most common his and hers items were sets of pillowcases and hand towels produced for the mass-market with the words "His and Hers," "Mr. and Mrs.," or "Guys and Dolls" embroidered on them. They were often embellished with flowers. We have also seen an unusual pair of printed towels by Tammis Keefe with the words Thine and Mine. Items without either the words His and Hers, Mr. and Mrs., Thine and Mine, or Guys and Dolls in the design, such as the couple on the bicycle built for two (Item 10.2) seen on this page, are uncommon. In this latter type of design, one towel is clearly masculine while the other is feminine. Most humorous and anthropomorphic designs similar to the ones included in this chapter date to the "fun linen period." His and hers designs executed before and after this period tended to be quite traditional.

Printed his and hers towels were also manufactured for the mass market; however, they never gained much popularity. Printed towels usually had interesting themes. One of the most unusual sets we have seen is Item 10.8 by Georges Briard. This towel set is an excellent example of anthropomorphic design. Mr. Briard omitted the words His and Hers from this set of poodle towels, which was gift-boxed and sold as a bathroom ensemble with matching drinking glasses.

Many his and hers towels and pillowcases were made as home craft projects. Transfer patterns and sets with pre-printed designs ready to be embroidered were used to make most home projects. Many of the pre-printed sets included thread. Both transfer patterns and sets are available in the marketplace today.

His and hers hand towels and pillowcases were popular wedding, engagement, and bridal shower gifts especially during the "fun linen period." Most couples during this period began married life with one or more matching sets. Fun designs similar to those on the towels (Item 10.3) and the pillowcases (Item 10.5) were popular as "gag" gifts at bridal showers.

Because his and hers hand towels and pillowcases enjoyed enormous popularity during the mid-20th century, we often refer to them as home fashion fads of the '50s. It is possible this fad was driven by concern for sanitary conditions. For example, since the mid-1930s scientists had been expressing concerns about the use of handkerchiefs spreading germs; therefore, throughout the "fun linen period" the use of handkerchiefs was decreasing. Mass marketing of Kleenex in newspaper and magazine ads was definitely a factor in making the American public aware of sanitary issues. Perhaps a germ conscious society needed his and hers towels and pillowcases as well as paper tissues.

His and hers themes were also used on kitchen towels and aprons during the "fun linen period." They were not usually sold in sets. They were almost always purchased separately. These items were less popular than hand towels and pillowcases. Consequently, they are more difficult to find.

There are large numbers of his and hers items available on the vintage linen market today. Most of them are unsigned and, for the most part, they are not particularly appealing to collectors unless they have fun themes. For example, ordinary his and hers hand towel sets sell for $10 to $15 while towel sets with fun themes are in the $30 to $60 price range. The his and hers kitchen towels (Item 10.10) and crying towels (Item 10.6) in this chapter are currently very collectible. Ordinary pillowcases sell for $8 to $35 per pair while the price range on fun pillowcases is $35 to $80 per pair. We have also included two unusual and very desirable examples of fun pillowcases (Items 10.5 and 10.9). It should be noted that while some collectors purchase his and hers towels or pillowcases separately, the pairs are worth more than one individual his or hers towel or pillowcase.

The idea of his and hers has left its mark in the marketplace. Hand towels, full size bath towels, and bathrobes are being manufactured today. A brief search on the Internet reveals numerous web sites where they can be purchased. As noted above, transfer patterns and craft sets are also available by mail order. It is interesting to note that the new his and hers items and the transfer patterns we have seen are traditional in design. New items and patterns with fun designs do not appear to be available.

10.2 Description: Appliquéd Bicycle Built for Two Hand Towels
The charming couple in old-fashioned clothing is enjoying a ride on their bicycle built for two. The design is unusual and the hand appliqué is very well done. His and hers is not embroidered on the towel. Unfortunately, the set is faded from repeated washing. We consider it to be in poor condition.
Measurements: 25"L x 12.75"W
Price Range:
$30-40 pair
$10-15 pair, poor condition

10.3 *Description:* Appliquéd Naughty His and Hers Guest Towels
This set of towels could easily be placed in the next chapter featuring naughty linen.
It is collectible both as a piece of his and hers linen and as a piece of naughty linen.
The woman has padded breasts and the gentleman has a padded derrière. The
woman's pants are on the floor. This set of towels is faded from repeated washing. We
consider it to be in poor condition.
Measurements: 18.25"L x 13.25"W
Price Range:
$40-45 pair
$10-15 pair, poor condition

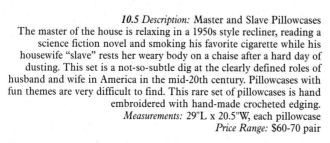

10.4 *Description:* His Apron
"It's So Nice to Have a Man Around the House" is printed at the
bottom of this bright red apron. The happy couple's clothing is
reminiscent of the 1950s. Since most men worked while women
took care of the home in the 1950s, we are not sure how many
men actually helped in the kitchen even though the man in this
apron is pictured busily washing dishes while his wife "beams" at
him. The man's apron states it is HIS apron in big bold letters. It
is likely this was meant to be a "gag" gift.
Measurement: 18.5"L x 25"W, gathered at the waist
Price Range: $10-12

10.5 *Description:* Master and Slave Pillowcases
The master of the house is relaxing in a 1950s style recliner, reading a
science fiction novel and smoking his favorite cigarette while his
housewife "slave" rests her weary body on a chaise after a hard day of
dusting. This set is a not-so-subtle dig at the clearly defined roles of
husband and wife in America in the mid-20th century. Pillowcases with
fun themes are very difficult to find. This rare set of pillowcases is hand
embroidered with hand-made crocheted edging.
Measurements: 29"L x 20.5"W, each pillowcase
Price Range: $60-70 pair

10.6 *Description:* Mom and Pop Crying Towels
These hand-painted towels were purchased separately and were usually not sold together as sets. They list many of the common complaints husbands and wives have about married life. For example, he seems concerned because she has purchased a new dress. She is concerned because whenever she wants something done she has to do it herself.
Measurements: 28"L x 17"W, each towel
Price Range: $20-22 each

10.7 *Description:* Appliquéd His and Hers Dog Towels
We are not sure what breed of puppy is pictured on his towel but the other dog appears to be a Dalmatian. The two pups are having a great time tugging at their respective towels. The appliqué work is well done and the canine subject matter is highly collectible and difficult to find in his and hers guest towel sets.
Measurements: 20"L x 12"W, each towel
Price Range: $50-60 pair

10.8 *Description:* His and Hers Poodle Towels, Georges Briard
The male poodle on the His towel is shaving while the beribboned female is applying powder to her face with a powder puff on the Hers towel. This set is signed by Georges Briard. It was also made with a white background. The retail price of this set of guest towels with the matching drinking glasses was $5 in the 1950s. The set was a very popular shower gift.
Measurements: 19"L x 12"W, each towel
Price Range: $30-35 pair

10.9 *Description:* His and Hers Pillowcases
This difficult to find set of hand-embroidered pillowcases shows two very well-dressed poodles in their lounge clothes looking in the mirror.
Measurements: 28"L x 21"W
Price Range: $45-55

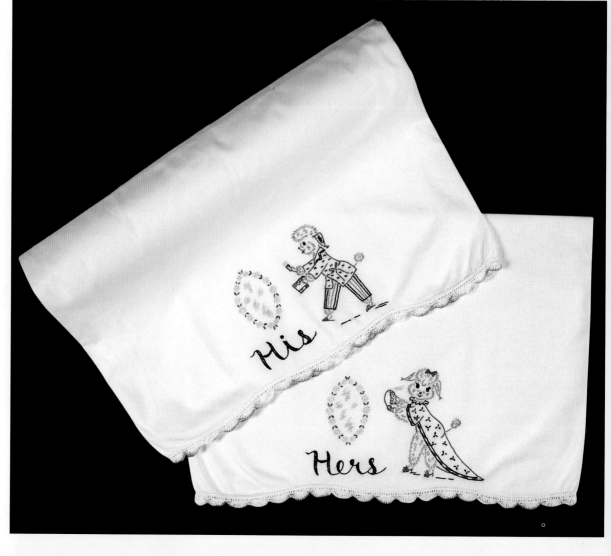

10.10 *Description:* It's a Dog's Life Kitchen Towels
A humorous take on a homemaker's day! These two
towels depict dogs doing a multitude of household
chores with the words "It's a Dog's Life" in the
center. The His version shows a masculine looking
gray dog mournfully washing a mountain of dishes.
The Hers version, which was also made in a red and
yellow color combination, shows a feminine looking
poodle in a frilly apron toiling over a hot stove. The
semi-comatose dog at the bottom of this page is
Princess Roo, one of Peggy's Rottweilers, who was
simply exhausted after viewing her fellow canines
working so hard on these two towels.
Measurements:
26"L x 15"W, Her Towel
28"L x 17"W, His Towel
Price Range: $25-30 each towel

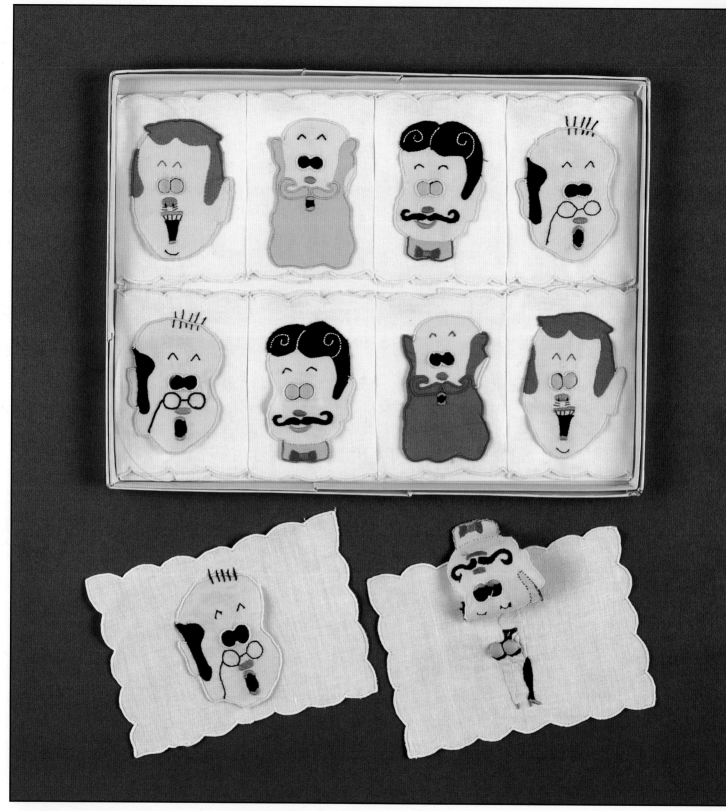

11.1 Description: Appliquéd Gentlemen's Faces Cocktail Napkins
The gentlemen's faces on these napkins appear rather odd at first glance.
Their eyes are bulging! When you lift the faces, you discover ladies
undressing underneath. It turns out that the bulging eyes are part of the
ladies' anatomies. Although currently considered politically incorrect, this
set is guaranteed to be a conversation piece at any party! Eight of the
napkins are seen in their original box. Two napkins from a second set are
open and arranged below the box. This set is very collectible.
Measurements: 4.75"L x 6.5"W
Price Range: $100-150 set of eight

106

Chapter 11
Naughty

Naughty household linen was very popular in America during the "fun linen period." It is logical to wonder why this type of household linen became popular in this country at a time when moral family life was at it peak. One would think it would have been the rage in other parts of the world where sexual values differed from those of America. Admittedly, when we first saw examples of naughty household linen we assumed it had originated and been popular in Europe before migrating to America. To our surprise, this initial premise was not confirmed by our research. We discovered that most of the household linen in this chapter was made specifically for the American market after World War II and into the 1960s. We have been unable to uncover information indicating that naughty household linen was popular in any other country at any time after the war until the present time.

Several obvious phenomena that occurred during World War II contributed to the rise in popularity of naughty household linen in America: pinup girls appearing in shows in USO canteens, pinup calendars, the American servicemen's exposure to European culture, and the changing role of American women who were filling the void left in the workforce in America or serving in the armed forces.

Pinup calendars were found everywhere from bomber planes to submarines. They were accepted and encouraged as a means of raising the morale of the American troops. Many Americans still remember Betty Grable, who starred in the movie *Pin Up Girl* in 1944, posing for pinup calendars. It is often said that she had the most famous pair of legs in World War II. We also remember scenes from movies of American troops enjoying performances in USO canteens and servicemen in Europe, particularly France, enjoying themselves while on leave. We have a set of cocktail napkins picturing service-

men on leave in this chapter (Item 11.2). The role of American women, sometimes pictured in blue jeans, working in factories is also well documented.

It is interesting to note the popularity of naughty linen in America at the same time that the classic television series *Leave It To Beaver* (in production from 1957 to 1963) was attracting large viewing audiences every week. The popularity of naughty linen juxtaposed against the Cleavers, who epitomized the traditional mid-20th century American family, highlights the enormous change taking place in American society during this period. On the one hand, moral family life in America was at its peak with the baby boom, the divorce rate at half of what it is today, home ownership skyrocketing, and the single-breadwinner middle-class family emblematic of post World War II prosperity. On the other hand, public discussion of sex, which would have been frowned upon earlier in the century, was becoming more acceptable.

Playboy magazine debuted on the American scene in December 1953 with tremendous fanfare. Marilyn Monroe was the centerfold in the first issue and *Playboy* eventually became the largest-selling and most influential men's magazine in the world. Playboy clubs began opening across America in 1960 and the number of "keyholders" eventually swelled to 1,000,000.

As discussions about sex became more open, fun household linen designs reflected this new social phenomenon. Americans were adding hide-a-bars in their homes and cocktails before dinner were in vogue. As demand grew for fun linen for entertaining, the supply of naughty linen increased accordingly. Cocktail napkins, guest towels, and bar towels were the most popular items produced.

Many of the examples of household linen in this chapter depict scantily clad ladies. Other examples have ladies with skirts that lift to reveal their legs. Many of the best quality examples of this type of household linen were appliqué, produced in Madeira for the American market. Household linen showing ladies with padded breasts and/or derrières was particularly popular. We sometimes refer to them as 3-D linen. It should be noted that we have seen very few examples of household linen depicting men with padded derrières. Household linen from this genre was used mainly for entertaining.

A few items in this chapter were made before the "fun linen period." They are the Appenzell-type placemats and runner (Item 11.19), which were made in the first quarter of the twentieth century; and the Italian cutwork tablecloth (Item 11.7), which was likely to have been made in the early 1940s. At the time these pieces were made, they would have been considered quite risqué and they probably had a fairly limited market. This may explain the scarcity of naughty household linen produced before World War II in today's marketplace.

11.2 Description: On Leave Cocktail Napkins Folder
Four napkins from a set of eight are pictured here with their original folder. Each of the napkins in the set has a different scene. The eight scenes depict enlisted men from the armed services enjoying various activities while on leave during World War II. On two of the napkins not pictured here, there are sailors talking on the phone and soldiers eyeing a burlesque show. One of the napkins has a large hole and many of the others are heavily stained. We purchased this set in this condition because of its unusual subject matter. The same set in good condition would be collectible.
Measurements: 7.125"L x 5.25"W each napkin
Price Range:
$65-75 set of eight in folder
$20-25 set of eight, poor condition

It would be difficult to discuss naughty household linen from the 20th century without mentioning Mae West. When Mae West, one of the best-known "naughty" ladies in 20th century pop culture, wrote and co-produced a play aptly named *Sex* in 1926, both she and the play became the target of censorship groups such as the Society for the Suppression of Vice. The police actually arrested the cast. Mae West was found guilty of corrupting the morals of the youth and sentenced to ten days in a New York City jail. We have included a hand-embroidered towel depicting Mae West uttering her famous line "Come up and see me sometime" in this chapter (Item 11.11).

Appenzell-type household linen, similar to the set shown in this chapter, is the most collectible naughty household linen from the early 20th century. In terms of the "fun linen period," the most collectible pieces are the 3-D cocktail napkins and guest towels.

Naughty household linen is still being made today and Elizabeth has seen new cocktail napkins and guest towels similar to those pictured as Items 11.14 and 11.16 being sold in high-end linen shops in Florence, Rome, and London during the past three years. When she discussed the market for these household linens in Italy and England with various shopkeepers, they told her they carried the lines with the intent of selling them to American tourists. They confirmed that this type of household linen was never very popular with Europeans.

It is interesting to note that naughty themes were never popular as subject matter for handkerchiefs in the 20th century. There are only two examples of naughty handkerchiefs in this chapter (Item 11.10). We have very few naughty handkerchiefs in our collections and this is due to lack of availability. Since naughty themes appealed primarily to male audiences, it is possible that the scarcity of naughty handkerchiefs was due to the fact that the bulk of fun handkerchiefs in the 20th century were made for women or children.

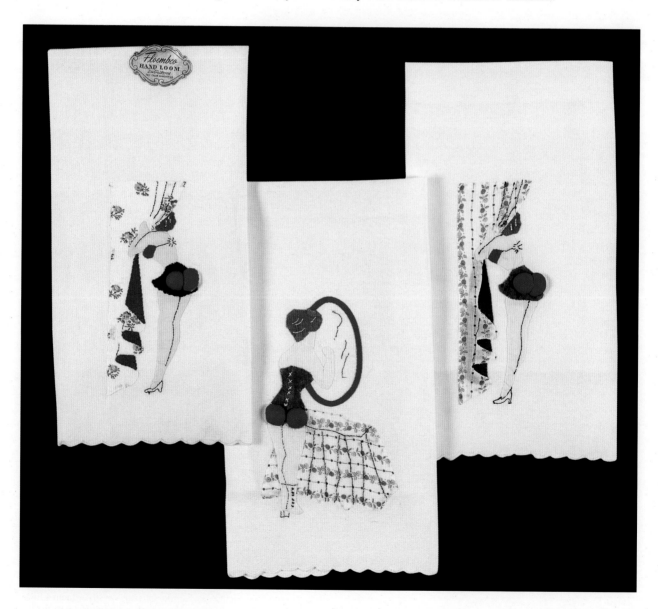

11.3 Description: Appliquéd Ladies Guest Towels
Scantily clad ladies with padded derrières adorn these three towels. Different floral materials were used for the curtains and dressing table skirts. One of the towels retains its original paper label that reads "Floembco, Hand Loom, Embroidered, Fast Color Guaranteed." The scalloped border is on only one end of the towels.
Measurements: 18.5"L x 10.5"W
Price Range: $25-28 each towel

11.4 *Description:* Appliquéd Pinup Girls Towels and Table Cover
The designs on these three towels are from a set of transfer patterns, which were sold by
Vogart Company. The cover from the Vogart pattern set is also shown on this page. We have
only three of the eight towels from the set. The entire set is very difficult to find and we have
never seen a complete set for sale. The towels are shown with a table cover, which has the
same pattern as one of the towels. This particular pattern is called "Pin Up Girls" and "Gay
Ninety Misses." The Vogart cover states that you can embroider or appliqué the patterns as
you wish. It suggests using padding under the panties and bra to shape them a little if you
appliqué them. The ladies on the towels do not have padding. The pinup on the table cover
is padded.
Vogart Cover: *Collection of Kathy Scherffius*
Measurements:
25.5"L x 17.5"W, towels
36" square, table cover
Price Range:
$25-30 each towel
$35-40 table cover

11.5 Description: Ladies Behind Keyholes
Cocktail Napkins
*Four different ladies are seen undressing
behind keyholes. Four other ladies from this
set of eight napkins are not pictured. Could
there be a "Peeping Tom" who isn't seen here?
This set of napkins is in poor condition with
small holes on three of the examples pictured.*
Measurements: 5.25"L x 7.25"W
Price Range:
$60-65 set of eight
$16-18 set of eight, poor condition

11.6 Description: Appliquéd Ladies Behind Keyholes Cocktail Napkins
Four cocktail napkins from a set of eight with scantily dressed ladies behind
old-fashioned keyholes are shown. There are four different poses in the set
of eight and each pose is repeated in different colors. The second set of eight
napkins shown here features similar ladies. This second set is still sewn to a
cardboard back and the original paper label reads "Paragon Needlecraft,
Hand Embroidery, Madeira." The napkins are hand embroidered on linen.
Padded circles were used for the ladies' breasts and derrières. This set is
very collectible. There is definitely something very naughty about watching
ladies dress through keyholes.
Measurements: 5"L x 8"W
Price Range: $75-100 set of eight

11.7 *Description:* Cutwork Ladies Tablecloth
Buxom naked ladies adorn this cutwork tablecloth made in Italy in the second quarter of the 20th century. There are three pairs of cherubs on either end of the tablecloth and two cutwork flowers on each side. The oval cutwork panel going around the center of the tablecloth is filled with cherubs and flowers. There are four large cherubs holding bunches of grapes on the ends and two pairs of cherubs with a horn on both sides. The design of the tablecloth is cheerful and fun. The workmanship is average.
Measurements: 97"L x 64"W
Price Range: $90-100

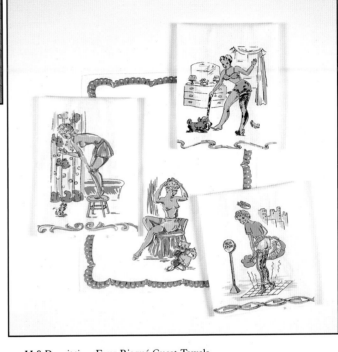

11.8 *Description:* Four Risqué Guest Towels
The four towels appear to be from a series. A lady is printed on one end of each towel. Two of the ladies on the towels are enjoying playing with their animals. A third lady is on a stool fearful of the mouse on the floor with his hands on his hips. Are the fish on the shower curtain looking at her? The final lady is at a bus stop and air from the street grate is blowing up her skirt. This is reminiscent of Marilyn Monroe's unforgettable pose with her white skirt flying up as she stood over a subway grate in the 1955 movie, *The Seven-Year Itch.*
Measurements: 18.25"L x 15.5"W
Price Range: $25-30 each towel

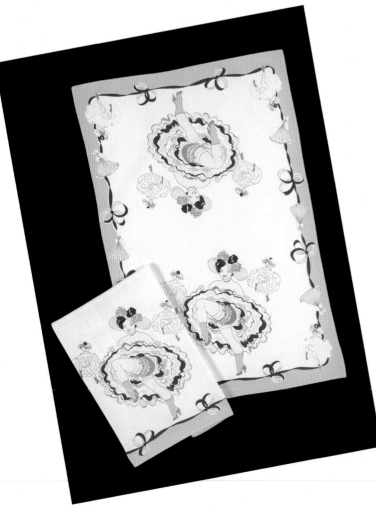

11.9 *Description:* Cancan Dancer Towels
Cancan dancers are printed on both ends of the towel. The scene is reminiscent of the Moulin Rouge in Paris. Paris scenes were popular on naughty linen.
Measurements: 26.5"L x 17.5"W
Price Range: $25-30 each towel

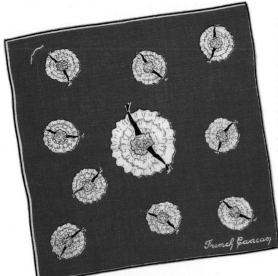

11.10 Description: Cancan Handkerchiefs
The scenes are in Paris and the cancan dancers are kicking their heels so high up in the air that their petticoats obscure their faces. Each handkerchief has "French Cancan" written on the bottom right-hand corner. The paper label on one handkerchief reads "*Bloch Frères.*" They are likely to have been a souvenir from a trip to Paris, France. Paris had a certain allure for Americans during the "fun linen period." Many American servicemen returning from Europe after World War II had experienced the French culture during the war and it became a favorite destination for Americans who traveled to Europe during the postwar years.
Measurements: 13" square, each handkerchief
Price Range: $25-30 each

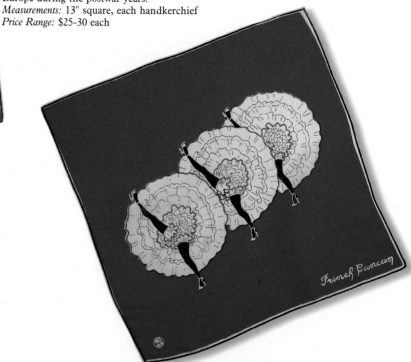

11.11 Description: Mae West Towel
Mae West was a 20th century American actress who was well known for her flashy, tight-fitting clothing and provocative remarks. She made the phrase "Come up and see me sometime" famous in 1928 when she starred in the play *Adamant Lil*, which she also wrote. *She Done Him Wrong*, the film adaptation, was produced in 1933 starring Mae opposite a young Cary Grant. The famous phrase was uttered again by W.C. Fields to Mae West in the film *My Little Chickadee* in 1940. This towel is hand embroidered with a hand-made crocheted border. The Mae West figure is on one end of the towel. The subject matter makes this towel collectible.
Measurements: 27"L x 18"W
Price Range: $20-25

11.12 Description: Appliquéd Ladies Kicking Up Their Skirts Napkins
The naughty appliquéd ladies posing and dancing around a cocktail shaker take us back to the days of saloons. The two ladies in blue and red bring back memories of Mae West. Six napkins from a set of eight are shown. The ladies appear in four different poses.
Measurements: 4.75"L x 6.75"W
Price Range: $75-100 set of eight

11.13 *Description:* Appliquéd Proper Ladies Cocktail Napkins
Is this a set of eight cocktail napkins with proper ladies? Look twice before you decide. All of the ladies have skirts that lift. This set of napkins is difficult to find and very collectible.
Measurements: 5"H x 6.75"W
Price Range: $75-100 set of eight

11.14 *Description:* Appliquéd Ladies
Linen Towels
Four scantily dressed ladies are seen on the towels. One lady has dropped her mirror. The other three are in various stages of undressing. Two of the scenes are similar to those in Item 11.17. The workmanship is very good. However, the towels are noticeably faded.
Measurements: 18.5"L x 11.5"W
Price Range:
$75-80 set of four
$25-30 set of four, poor condition

11.15 *Description:* Appliquéd Lady Dropping Her Drawers Towel
An appliquéd linen towel depicting a lady caught in an embarrassing moment dropping her drawers is shown here. This is yet another amusing 3-D towel.
Measurements: 18"L x 12.5"W
Price Range: $30-35

11.16 Description: Appliquéd Naughty Ladies Cocktail Napkins
Each of the eight cocktail napkins above has a different scene. The napkin with the lady on the phone is very unusual. The napkins are in their original box and the original label is still attached to the set. It reads "Paragon Needlecraft, Hand Embroidery, Madeira." These napkins are very collectible.
Measurements: 5"L x 7"W
Price Range: $100-125 set of eight

11.17 Description: Appliquéd Ladies and a Gentleman Cocktail Napkins
This set of six appliquéd napkins shows five ladies and a gentleman. The gentleman and the lady on the middle two napkins are ready for bed. They match the towels in Item 11.18. Ladies who are undressing or undressed are on the other four napkins. Two of them seem to be in distress. One is having great difficulty since she has encountered a mouse watching her. Another lady has broken her mirror. We hope she isn't superstitious.
Measurements: 6.75"L x 4.75"W
Price: $65-75 set of six

11.18 Description: Appliquéd Men and Women in Nightclothes Guest Towels
Two pairs of appliquéd linen guest towels showing a bedtime scene from the turn of the century are pictured here. The male in red long johns and nightcap is holding his evening candlestick while the female with braided blond hair in a red nightgown holds her candle. The man and woman on the second pair of towels are in identical poses; however, they are holding lamps instead of candles. The ladies have padded breasts while the men have padded derrières. The workmanship on both sets is good.
Measurements: 20"L x 12"W, each towel
Price Range: $45-50 each pair

11.19 Description: Appenzell-type Figural Placemats and Runner
This set includes eleven early 20th century hand-embroidered linen placemats and a matching runner. Each of the placemats has a hand-embroidered figure in the center of a medallion with a pulled thread mesh background. A partially clad male figure is on five of the placemats while six others have a nude dancing lady. There is hemstitching throughout the center and a scrolling punch work mosaic pattern interspersed with floral rosettes all along the border. The runner has figural medallions on both ends. One medallion depicts the same male and female figure pictured on the placemats dancing together. The other medallion depicts a partially clad couple in a different dance pose. Each piece in the set bears the monogram IWH. All eleven placemats are in excellent condition. Unfortunately, the runner has several holes and two badly repaired tears in the center. This rather risqué design is atypical for Appenzell-type embroidery. In household linen, the vast majority of this type of embroidery depicts courting couples in period costume or maidens in period costume in bucolic settings. This set is very unusual and very collectible.
Measurements:
50.25"L x 17.5"W, runner
11.5"L x 28"W, each placemat
Price Range: $1,250-1,500 twelve-piece set

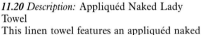

11.20 Description: Appliquéd Naked Lady Towel
This linen towel features an appliquéd naked lady with her back to us. She is partially covered by a layer of appliquéd bubbles. We have not seen another example of this towel.
Measurements: 19.75"L x 13.125"W
Price Range: $30-35

11.21 Description: Come and Get It Apron
This hand-painted apron may never have been used. The paint does not show any sign of flaking or cracking. We have not tried to wash this apron, and we assume that the paint would eventually be damaged after repeated washing. The names Ethel and Don are in a different type of print from that used for the phrase "Come and Get It." This leads us to believe that the two names were probably added later. This type of item was popular as a humorous gift.
Measurements: 33.5"L x 26"W
Price Range: $20-25

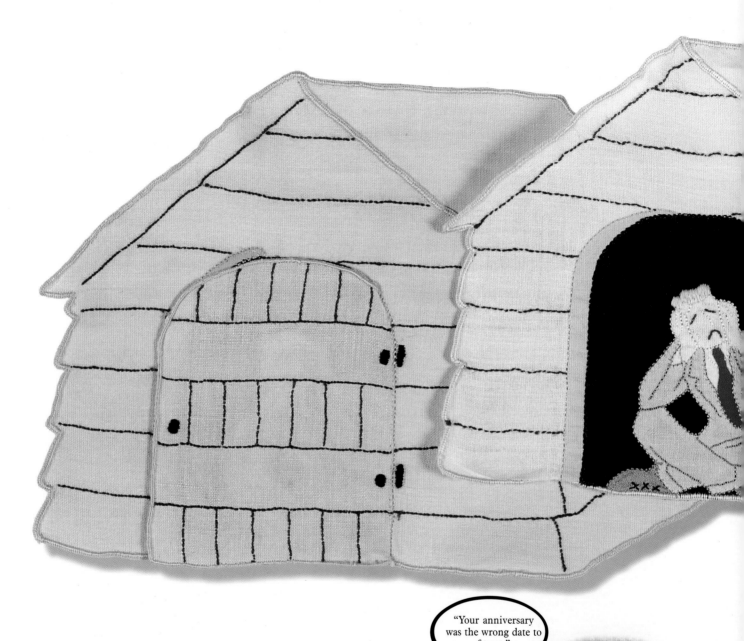

"Your anniversary was the wrong date to forget."

12.1 Description: Appliquéd Man in a Doghouse Cocktail Napkins, and Man's Best Friend Looking Confused

Each of the amusing and unusual napkins shown here is from a set of eight. The napkins were made in two different colors, white and yellow, and they are very collectible in either color. They are in the shape of a doghouse, which has a door that opens to reveal a man in a business suit. The details of the man's face are so complete that his morose mood comes through very clearly. He is literally in the doghouse. The dog on this page is Mac, one of Peggy's Rottweilers. He is very confused by the men on the napkins. Until he saw each of us buy a set of these napkins, he thought doghouses were for dogs. The pieces are hand embroidered and the quality of the workmanship and the material is very good. There are round paper labels that read "Linen, Madeira, Portugal" on the backs of the yellow napkins.

Photography Credit: *Photograph of Mac by Alice Su*
Measurements: 5"L x 7.75"W
Price Range: $125-150 set of eight, either color

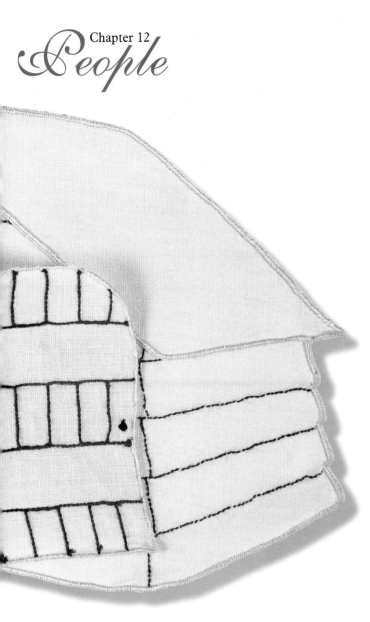

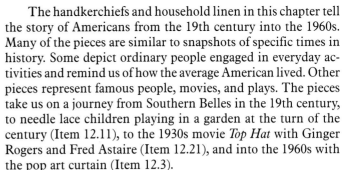

The handkerchiefs and household linen in this chapter tell the story of Americans from the 19th century into the 1960s. Many of the pieces are similar to snapshots of specific times in history. Some depict ordinary people engaged in everyday activities and remind us of how the average American lived. Other pieces represent famous people, movies, and plays. The pieces take us on a journey from Southern Belles in the 19th century, to needle lace children playing in a garden at the turn of the century (Item 12.11), to the 1930s movie *Top Hat* with Ginger Rogers and Fred Astaire (Item 12.21), and into the 1960s with the pop art curtain (Item 12.3).

The topic of people on household linen and handkerchiefs was very popular in the 20th century and there are many examples in excellent and good condition available. Some of the pieces we first considered for inclusion in this chapter migrated to other chapters. For example, pieces with people eating, drinking, going to the circus, undressing, engaging in sports, and traveling were placed in other more appropriate chapters. The topic of people is similar to animals since it could have been the topic for an entire book. As they said at the beginning of the famous television show *Candid Camera*, "People are Funny."

Some of the designs featured in the chapter are extremely fanciful, and based on stereotypes as opposed to actual people. The printed tablecloth with matching napkins made by Fodor (Item 12.31) is a wonderful example of this. The design is called "Wedding Bells" and features a whole host of characters that resemble escapees from an old B-movie. The half-naked, extremely tipsy sister and the mustachioed bridegroom (who really reminds us of the villain in the *Perils of Pauline*) are particularly outstanding.

As America moved forward at an increasingly fast pace in the 20th century, Americans took great pleasure in occasional nostalgic glimpses back to America's past. The motifs on several items in this chapter take us back to the 19th century. Some examples of household linen reminiscent of the past include: the appliquéd tablecloth with a couple in Victorian costume posing before a camera and the Southern Belle pillowcases, apron, and towels.

Household linen and handkerchiefs featuring famous people are probably the most desirable collectibles featured in this chapter. For instance, Fred Astaire and Ginger Rogers fans, movie and entertainment memorabilia buffs, and handkerchief collectors are likely to find the *Top Hat* handkerchief pictured as Item 12.21 of great interest. Items signed by famous designers such as the Rich Man, Poor Man handkerchiefs (Item 12.30) signed by Pat Prichard and Carl Tait respectively are also highly desirable collectibles. And finally, unusual and humorous designs, such as the man in the doghouse cocktail napkins (Item 12.1) and the "How to" handkerchiefs (Item 12.6) often command high prices in today's marketplace.

12.2 Description: **Blondie** Handkerchief
Blondie was a popular comic strip created by Chic Young in 1930. J.J. Murphy's book *Children's Handkerchiefs, A Two Hundred Year History* describes *Blondie* as a comic strip that "gradually developed into a domestic comedy of middle class life" in America. The 1940s children's handkerchief pictured here features the entire Bumstead family: Blondie, Dagwood, Alexander, Cookie, Daisy, and her pups. There are a number of different handkerchiefs from the 1940s based on the *Blondie* comic strip. They are all collectible.
Measurements: 8.5"L x 8"W
Price Range: $30-40

12.3 Description: Your Own Thing Curtains
The teenagers on this curtain are doing their own thing. The curtain is an example of 1960s pop art household linen. The teenagers are surfing, kissing, and dancing. Love is written across the curtain various times. Favorite sayings of this time period are printed on the curtain. A close-up of a section of the curtain is also seen on this page. The close-up features one of the favorite sayings of the time, "It's bigger than both of us." The curtain is one of a pair.
Measurements: 80"L x 39"W, each curtain panel
Price Range: $75-100 pair

12.4 Description: Sweet Stuff Handkerchief
This handkerchief brings back memories of teenagers in the 1950s and reminds us of Archie and his gang. Many of our readers will remember going to the local diner or drugstore after school to drink Cokes and eat sundaes. "The Original Bait'em, E.W. Eldridge Co." is printed on the paper label in the right-hand corner. The label covers the initials T.E.L. An identical sticker and these initials are also on the handkerchief in Item 12.5. In addition to the two handkerchiefs, we have seen these initials on three other handkerchiefs. The scenes on the other three are: teenagers dancing with the words "Jive Music" printed across the middle; a teenage couple dressed for the prom surrounded by traffic signs that read "Stop, Go, Caution, S.O.S."; and a boy and a girl talking on the telephone surrounded by hearts with the words "Party Line" printed above them. It is possible that there are more handkerchiefs in this series. All five of these designs utilize this eye-catching blue, green, red, and yellow color combination.
Measurements: 12.25"L x 12.5"W
Price Range: $35-40 for each handkerchief

12.5 Description: Crusin' Handkerchief

This handkerchief is part of a series as noted on the previous page. It is also reminiscent of the 1950s. The young men on this handkerchief are riding around picking up young women. The car has "capacity six girls" painted on the rear door. Currently, there is room for one more. "Don't laugh Mother your daughter may be inside!!" is painted on the hood of the car. "Crusin for a brusin" is painted on the car's rear fender. This was a very popular 1950s saying. The original price tag, which reads "J.C. PENNEY CO., 15 cents," is still on the handkerchief.

Measurements: 12.25"L x 12.5"W
Price Range: $35-40

12.6 Description: How to Get a Husband Handkerchief and How to Keep Your Husband Handkerchief

The two handkerchiefs give advice in English, Spanish, and French to both married and single women. They are great conversation pieces and evoke many groans from women and cheers from the men. Read the advice and decide for yourself how accurate (or inaccurate) these handkerchiefs really are!

Measurements:
13.25"L x 13"W, How to Get a Husband
12.75" square, How to Keep Your Husband
Price Range: $50-65 each handkerchief

12.7 Description: Crying Handkerchief

Crying towels are fairly common. However, crying handkerchiefs are very unusual. The young ladies pictured here seem impossible to please. This handkerchief was printed in Spain.

Measurements: 14"L x 14.5"W
Price Range: $35-40

12.8 Description: O.K. Dear – Wear the Curlers Pillowcase
This white cotton pillowcase is all hand embroidered with handmade tatting attached to the border. Even though this is only a single pillowcase, Peggy simply couldn't resist this particular scene. She often purchases interesting single pillowcases for her collection and frequently mixes and matches them for use in her home. However, since most people prefer to use matching pairs, single pillowcases typically sell at a significant discount.
Measurements: 30"L x 21"W
Price Range:
$30-35 single pillowcase
$80-85 pair of pillowcases

12.9 Description: Persian Series, Tammis Keefe
Tammis Keefe repeatedly used Persian themes in her textile designs. Her first Persian inspired design was for a furnishing fabric called "Persian Horses" that was produced and marketed by Goodall Fabrics. This company had showrooms and wholesale operations on Madison Avenue in New York City during the mid-20th century. "Persian Horses" proved to be extremely popular. In 1944 it was used for the curtains in the guest rooms at the Hotel New Yorker in New York City and in 1946 for the curtains at the Somerset Hotel in Boston. Tammis Keefe subsequently designed a series of at least five linen handkerchiefs for J.H. Kimball and Company in the 1950s with variations on this Persian theme. This theme also appears on a set of cocktail napkins and several Tammis Keefe towels and silk scarves. All Persian theme handkerchiefs are relatively easy to find. We have seen handkerchiefs in the Persian series with black, dark brown, navy blue, and dark green backgrounds. The black background seems to be the most collectible and easiest to find piece in the series. Both the Persians with Giraffes and the Persians in Garden handkerchiefs retain their original yellow and gold J. H. Kimball & Company paper labels. The first handkerchief also has its original Lord & Taylor price tag indicating it sold for $1. This was quite expensive for a handkerchief in those days. In comparison, the Crusin' handkerchief pictured in Item 12.5 retailed in the same time period for 15 cents. Although the Persians Playing Musical Instruments handkerchief pictured here is unsigned, it is part of the Keefe Persian series. We have signed examples identical to this handkerchief in our collections. The design is similar to some of the scenes on the cocktail napkins also shown here. We have seen a number of unsigned handkerchiefs from the Persian series presumably from an error in the printing process. Unsigned examples sell at a discount compared to signed examples.

Measurements:
29"L x 16"W, towels
7.75"L x 5.5"W, napkins
14.75"L x 15"W, each handkerchief
Price Range:
$35-40 towels in either color
$65-75 set of eight napkins in either color
$25-28 black, navy blue, and dark green, signed handkerchiefs
$18-21 dark brown, signed handkerchiefs
$15-20 unsigned handkerchiefs

12.10 *Description:* Appenzell-type Figural Round Linen Tablecloth
This charming tablecloth is completely hand embroidered with little girls covered with flowers dancing in a circle. The girls' dresses are formed with a combination of raised outlines and pulled thread work. The combination of the fine quality embroidery and the figural scenes make this tablecloth very desirable. Appenzell and Appenzell-type figural embroidery typically depicts adults in period costume. The subject matter on this tablecloth is unusual.
Measurements: 29" diameter; each little girl is 8.5" tall
Price Range: $150-175

12.11 *Description:* Needle Lace Doilies
These two figural doilies are handmade needle lace. They represent the type of high-end household linen that was popular at the turn of the century. The subject matter, children surrounded by flowers, is serene and representative of the time. The workmanship and design of these pieces is excellent.
Measurements: 6.5" diameter
Price Range: $175-225 pair

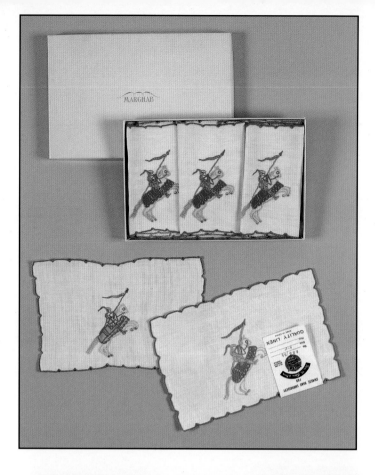

12.12 *Description:* Appliquéd Knight Cocktail Napkins, Marghab, and Appliquéd Knight Cocktail Napkins, China
The knight pattern shown here is one of the most readily found Marghab cocktail napkin patterns. These napkins are very collectible and always attract numerous bidders when they are sold at auction. The set pictured here is in unused condition and was found in its original Marghab box. The appliquéd figures and all the other embroidered areas were made by hand on linen. This motif was also made in green and yellow. The red version seems to be the most common; however, all four colors currently sell in the same price range. At a glance, the set of napkins on the bottom right could be mistaken for the Marghab set pictured above it. However, the original paper label on this set indicates it was made in China for another firm. This set could have easily been identified as a reproduction of Marghab even if the label had been absent. The quality of the linen is a very strong indication that it is not Marghab since they used very fine linen or organdy or a combination of both for all their patterns. The linen used in this set is considerably heavier and coarser. When the sets are side by side, it is apparent that there are subtle differences in the embroidery, particularly in the areas of the horse's rear legs and the pennant on the knight's lance. In addition, this set of napkins is larger than the original set.
Measurements:
4.75L x 7.75W, original Marghab napkin
5.5"L x 8.25"W, napkin made in China
Price Range:
$125-150 set of twelve Marghab napkins
$36-40 set of eight Chinese napkins

12.13 *Description:* Sunbonnet Girls, Days of the Week Towels
These towels are hand embroidered from a transfer pattern set. The girls have a different chore for every day of the week except Sunday, which is reserved for church. Because of the enduring popularity of Sunbonnet Girl patterns, this type of set is still being made today. We have seen Sunbonnet Girl days of the week transfer patterns dating as early as the 1930s. McCalls made some of the earliest patterns. Complete vintage towel sets from the 1930s, '40s, and '50s are difficult to find. The set pictured here is one of the later sets. It is likely this set is circa 1970. This set is attractive both to collectors of Sunbonnet Girls and collectors of days of the week items.
Measurements: 29.5"L x 14.5"W, each towel
Price Range:
$70-80 set of seven, vintage
$35-45 set of seven, 1970s

12.14 *Description:* Sunbonnet Lady Apron
Sunbonnet Ladies, Southern Belles, and Crinoline Ladies are all terms used to describe designs depicting ladies in period costume. These terms are used because the ladies all have huge sunbonnets and wide hoop skirts. These ladies appeared on all types of household linen as well as handkerchiefs. The lady in this apron is rather unusual because she is facing forward and her facial features are very detailed. Most sunbonnet ladies are shown in profile and their bonnets typically obscure their facial features. For a nice added touch to this apron, the lady's fan forms a pocket, which is useful for carrying a handkerchief or small items. The apron is hand embroidered and the apron's ties are hand finished. It was probably a home project.
Measurements: 28.5"L x 28.5"W
Price Range: $25-28

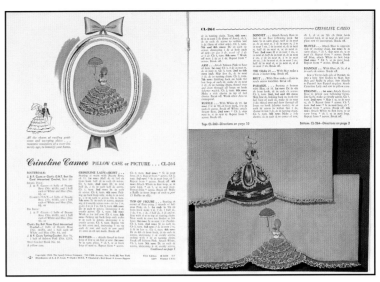

12.15 *Description:* Pair of Sunbonnet Lady Pillowcases
One from a pair of hand-embroidered pillowcases is shown here. The pattern on these pillowcases is similar to the pattern shown in an instruction pamphlet titled *Crinoline Lady in Crochet*, which was published in 1949 and also pictured here.
Measurements: 32"L x 19"W
Price Range: $30-32

12.16 *Description:* 1970 Calendar Towel
Two Sunbonnet Ladies are walking their poodles on the 1970 linen calendar towel shown here. The towel has its original paper label that reads "Victory K.B. Inc., All Linen, Made in Poland."
Measurements: 28"L x 17"W
Price Range: $10-12

12.17 *Description:* Black Americana Towels
This set of six hand-embroidered dishtowels depicts Black couples engaged in various enjoyable activities. It was made from a set of transfer patterns in the last quarter of the 20th century. The transfer patterns are vintage.
Measurements: 34" square, each towel
Price Range:
$85-95 set of six, vintage
$45-60 set of six, last quarter of the 20th century

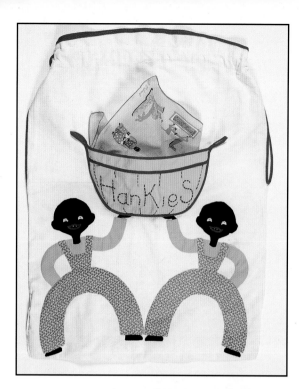

12.18 *Description:* Appliquéd Laundry Bag
This unique laundry bag has a special pouch sewn on the front. The pouch is designed to hold handkerchiefs. The appliqué on the bag is good quality and the design is very interesting. To date, this is the only example of this design we have seen. A handkerchief signed by Pat Prichard depicting scenes from a carnival is in the pocket of the laundry bag.
Measurements: 29"L x 21.5"W
Price Range: $35-45

12.19 *Description:* Little Girl Lipstick Towel The little child hand embroidered on this guest towel appears to have helped herself to more lipstick than she needs. She must be happy to know there is a lipstick towel in this powder room. Guest towels were very popular in the mid-20th century at a time when having a powder room in one's home was becoming an American status symbol.
Measurements: 14.25"L x 8"W
Price Range: $12-15

12.20 Description: Hello Dolly Handkerchiefs, Faith Austin
Both handkerchiefs depict Carol Channing in the starring role of Dolly in the play *Hello Dolly*. These cotton handkerchiefs are signed Faith Austin. Since the play that inspired these designs debuted on Broadway in 1964 with Ms. Channing originating the role of Dolly, we believe these handkerchiefs were produced circa 1965. One of the handkerchiefs still has three original paper tags. One tag reads "Franshaw Exclusive," the second tag says "Authentic Hello Dolly Design," and the last tag says "All Cotton R.N. 16153." As pictured here, one handkerchief is very similar to the scene on the back of the jacket of the original cast recording record while the other bears a close resemblance to the cover of the Playbill from the original Broadway production. A third handkerchief (not pictured) shows Dolly on a train to Yonkers. All three handkerchiefs are very difficult to find and highly collectible. Faith Austin also reproduced the Dolly on the staircase scene on a large silk scarf.

Hello Dolly is a musical based on the book *The Matchmaker* by Thornton Wilder. The music and lyrics for the play were by Jerry Herman, and Michael Steward wrote the book. The setting is New York City in 1890. It chronicles the many twists and turns of the romance between Dolly Gallagher Levi, well-known widowed matchmaker, and Horace Vandergelder, successful businessman. Of all the actresses who have played Dolly over the years, Ms. Channing is still considered by many to be the one most closely identified with the role. The original Broadway production ran for 2,844 performances and at one time held the record for the longest running Broadway production. Ms. Channing was succeeded in the role of Dolly by a long string of well-known actresses including Ginger Rogers, Martha Raye, Betty Grable, Bibi Osterwald, Pearl Bailey, Phyllis Diller, and Ethel Merman.
Measurements: 15" square, each handkerchief
Price Range:
$55-65 Dolly in the carriage
$50-60 Dolly on the staircase
$40-50 Dolly on the train

12.21 Description: Top Hat Handkerchief
This handkerchief is a wonderful piece of memorabilia for Ginger Rogers and Fred Astaire fans. It depicts the duo dancing the Piccolino, in the 1935 hit movie, *Top Hat*. This handkerchief was also made with blue, green, and turquoise backgrounds but the red background shown here is the most commonly found. This handkerchief may have been made as part of the promotional effort when the movie was first released in 1935. Although this example has two minor stains, the colors are bright and the fabric does not show any sign of wear. We would consider this handkerchief to be in good condition. It is difficult to find.
Measurements: 11.5" square
Price Range: $35-40 all four colors

12.22 Description: Lipstick Handkerchief
This is a very unusual lipstick handkerchief. The couple on the handkerchief reminds us of a European version of Ginger Rogers and Fred Astaire. The gentleman on the handkerchief is holding a sign that says "for your eyes." The lady has a sign that says "for your lips." Notice the bright red color on her lips.
Measurements: 13" square
Price Range: $40-50

12.23 *Description:* Four Dionne Quintuplets Handkerchiefs, Tom Lamb
Tom Lamb designed three of these four handkerchiefs in 1936 when
the quintuplets were two years old. The fourth handkerchief was
designed in 1937 when the girls were three years old. All four handkerchiefs are marked "Copyright NEA Service, Inc. and produced by the
J.C.W. Corporation." J.J. Murphy's book, *Children's Handkerchiefs: A
Two Hundred Year History*, states that Tom Lamb made at least six
different children's handkerchiefs featuring the Dionne Quintuplets.
All four of the handkerchiefs pictured here bear Tom Lamb's signature.
The first handkerchief shows the girls climbing stairs. It is in good
condition with a small rust stain near one edge. The second shows the
girls in purple polka dot dresses with little rabbits apparently conduct-
ing interviews with the girls. This handkerchief still has an original
paper label that reads, "made in Ireland." Unfortunately, Tom Lamb's
signature was printed poorly and is extremely faint. The third
handkerchief shows the five girls in pink and blue bonnets. It is in very
good condition. Of the four handkerchiefs this is the easiest to find.
The fourth handkerchief shows the girls engaged in various activities
such as playing the piano and pulling out one of three candles from
their birthday cake. It has a small hole and a damaged corner. Murphy's
book shows three of the four handkerchiefs pictured here in a different
color combination so we assume that all of the Dionne Quintuplets
handkerchiefs designed by Tom Lamb were made in at least two
different color versions. All four of these handkerchiefs are very
collectible and hard to find. They appeal to a wide range of collectors
including those interested in Dionne Quintuplets memorabilia, Tom
Lamb items, and children's handkerchiefs.

Tom Lamb also made at least one apron featuring the quintuplets. The
only example of this apron we have seen was in excellent condition and
sold for approximately $135 at an auction in June 2000.

The five girls, Emilie, Yvonne, Cecile, Maria, and Annette, were the
first documented set of quintuplets to survive for more than a few days
after birth. Born on May 28, 1934, in Ontario, Canada, the Dionne
Quintuplets became an instant sensation. In 1935 the Ontario
provincial government put the girls on display at Quintland, a theme
park like site, where the public was allowed to view them three times a
day through one-way glass windows. It was estimated that at the height
of their popularity over six thousand visitors viewed them per day.
Countless Quintuplets souvenirs in the form of dolls, calendars, playing
cards, handkerchiefs, spoons, and china were made and sold throughout the quintuplets' childhood years. Their images were also used in
numerous advertisements promoting various services or items such as
kitchen appliances.
Measurements: 8.75" square, each handkerchief
Price Range:
$60-70 first handkerchief
$70-75 second handkerchief
$40-55 third handkerchief
$65-75 fourth handkerchief
$25-35 fourth handkerchief, poor condition

12.24 Description: Butler and Maid Towel
The butler and maid on this towel are very properly dressed and busily carrying their trays. The butler seems to also be in charge of the family dog, a cute Scottish Terrier. Note the smiling face on the teapot the maid is carrying. Butler and maid motifs were popular on both printed and embroidered household linen in the mid-20th century.
Measurements: 27"L x 15.5"W
Price Range: $22-25

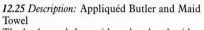

12.25 Description: Appliquéd Butler and Maid Towel
The butler and the maid are hand embroidered. The butler is carrying a tray with liquor and the maid is carrying a tray with tea. Her dress and his jacket are slightly faded.
Measurements: 29"L x 16.5"W
Price Range:
$25-30 good condition
$10-12 poor condition

12.26 Description: Lady with Handkerchief Dress
This is a very decorative gift box containing a handkerchief. The cover of the box seen to the left shows a lovely lady in a sheer pink dress walking in the grass. The inside of the box has the same scene except that the lady's dress is actually a sheer pink handkerchief.
Measurements: 7.125" square
Price Range: $12-15

12.27 *Description:* Appliquéd Victorian Couple Tablecloth
The couple on this unusual tablecloth is being photographed in Victorian clothing. This could actually be a Victorian couple or they could be in a booth where people dress in clothing from "the good old days" and have their photographs taken. The latter is the more likely scenario. The appliquéd scene with the couple and the photographer is shown on both ends. The appliqué work on the couple and the photographer is very good. A close-up photograph of the couple is also provided.
Measurements: 41"L x 35"W
Price Range: $45-50

12.28 *Description:* Embroidered People Runner
Male and female singers are hand embroidered on this damask runner. There are three women on the right-hand side of the runner and four men on the left-hand side. The quality of the embroidery is excellent.
Measurements: 41"L x 18"W
Price Range: $30-35

12.29 Description: Rich Man, Poor Man Cocktail Napkins Folder
This Leacock & Company, Inc. folder contains eight napkins hand printed on pure Irish linen. Each of the napkins has one of the characters from the children's rhyme *Rich Man, Poor Man* printed on it. Further details on the nursery rhyme are given with the next picture.
Measurements: 9.5"L x 57.5"W
Price Range: $45-55 set of eight in folder

12.30 Description: Rich Man, Poor Man Handkerchiefs, Pat Prichard and Carl Tait
Two linen handkerchiefs signed by Pat Prichard and one signed by Carl Tait are shown here. Each of the three handkerchiefs depicts a different version of the old children's rhyme *Rich Man, Poor Man.* According to the *Oxford Dictionary of Nursery Rhymes,* this was "a fortune-telling rhyme used when counting cherry stones, waistcoat buttons, daisy petals, or the seeds of the Timothy grass." For little boys, this was a way to guess what their future professions might be. For little girls, the rhyme supposedly predicted what type of man they would marry. Both the Prichard designs actually incorporate buttons and hearts pierced with arrows and retain their original J.H. Kimball & Company, Inc. paper labels. The Tait handkerchief retains its original Herrmann Handkerchief Company paper label as well as a round label indicating it was made with Irish linen. Both of the Prichard handkerchiefs retain their original Jordan Marsh Co. $1 price tags. All three handkerchiefs are difficult to find and highly collectible.
Measurements:
15"L x 14.75"W, Pat Prichard handkerchiefs
14.5" square, Carl Tait handkerchief
Price Range: $35-40 each of the three handkerchiefs

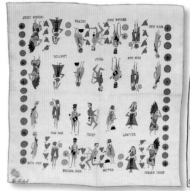

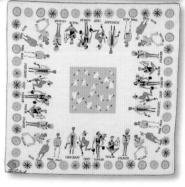

12.31 Description: Wedding Bells Tablecloth and Cocktail Napkins Set, Fodor
This printed tablecloth and napkin set is filled with "zany" characters. The lovely bride seems to be the only normal looking person at this wedding. The Happy Little Sister is kicking up her heels with such exuberance that she seems to have lost some of her clothing! The obligatory Weeping Mother is sobbing enough for everyone. Uncle Harry is singing loud enough to be heard in the next county, hopefully in tune. The Bridegroom looks more wicked than dashing with his luxuriant mustache and wolf's head cane. There are eight different characters in the tablecloth. It is signed in one corner "Pix Laszlo Fodor" and there is a cloth tag sewn into one hem that says "Styled by Dervan." The original cardboard folder with eight matching napkins is also pictured. Each napkin in the set has one of the eight characters from the tablecloth printed on it. The napkins are glued to the cardboard and would be difficult to remove without destroying the folder. The napkins have discolored around the glue. The folder itself is somewhat ragged around the edges. Each of the napkins is signed Fodor.
Measurements:
36"L x 31"W, tablecloth
8"L x 5.5"W, each napkin
Price Range:
$45-50 tablecloth
$30-35 napkins in the folder
$90-105 nine-piece set

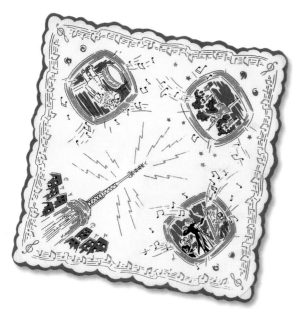

12.32 Description: Holiday Celebration Handkerchief
The three television screens in this handkerchief appear to be from the early days of television in the 1950s, which leads us to believe that this handkerchief dates to that period. The various scenes remind us of winter in New York City. The conductor and his orchestra evoke memories of Guy Lombardo, who was a fixture with his band at the Roosevelt Grill in New York City for over thirty years starting in 1929. Beginning in the 1950s, he and his band also appeared live on television on New Year's Eve for many years. The ice skating scene is reminiscent of scenes at the ice skating rink at Rockefeller Center in New York City. The red, green, and gold colors further reinforce the holiday season theme.
Measurements: 13.25"L x 13.5"W
Price Range: $12-15

12.33 Description: Umbrella-shaped Handkerchief
This is a very unusual handkerchief in the shape of an umbrella. The romantic scene features a couple silhouetted against the umbrella with rain coming down and birds flying overhead. A second umbrella-shaped handkerchief (not pictured) continues this romantic theme. It features a couple silhouetted against an umbrella as they sit on a park bench gazing into each other's eyes. Both handkerchiefs are difficult to find and highly collectible.
Measurements: 12.75" diameter
Price Range: $50-55 either handkerchief

12.34 Description: Blast Off Time Handkerchief
Americans had an enduring fascination with space and beings from outer space throughout the 20th century. Popular 20th century culture abounded with images of alien invasions of earth from cartoonist Alex Raymond's space hero, Flash Gordon, created in 1934, to Orson Welles' 1938 broadcast of *The War of Worlds*, to the 1990s hit television series *The X-Files*. Gene Roddenberry's *Star Trek* (which first aired on television in 1966) and George Lucas' *Star Wars* (first released in 1977) have expanded on the themes that we are not alone in the universe and that there is a great diversity of sentient species in outer space. America has been a leader in space exploration since the establishment of the National Aeronautics and Space Administration (NASA) in 1958. Many 20th century children dreamt of being astronauts; consequently, there were many space-theme toys, books, and other items made for children during the century. This children's handkerchief shows the crew boarding a space ship ready for blast off. It was also made in green. It is part of a series made in circa 1950.
Measurements: 13"H x 12.75"L
Price Range: $35-50

13.1 *Description:* Cowboy Tablecloth, Ivan Bartlett
There are very few Ivan Bartlett tablecloths. Of the few we have seen, this design is our favorite. It is the easiest to find and it is always popular with collectors at auction.
Measurements: 94"L x 51.5"W
Price Range: $75-100

Chapter 13
Southwest, South of the Border, and South American Influence

Prior to the "fun linen period" very little household linen was designed with southwestern themes. It is likely that this occurred because in the early part of the century the heat and humidity, lack of water supply, and the need for a highway system in the Southwestern states greatly hampered their development.

In the 1930s the construction of water sources such as Hoover Dam made it possible for the Southwestern states to increase their water supply and support larger populations. In 1927 the national highway system was formed. By 1937 Route 66 had been completed from Chicago to Santa Monica, California. It became one of the most famous highways in America. Jack Kerouac's book *On the Road* and Nat King Cole's song *Route 66* helped to immortalize it. The highway also inspired a television series, *Route 66*, which was in production from 1960 to 1964.

In the postwar prosperity automobile ownership increased and air conditioning became available. This resulted in large numbers of Americans traveling and vacationing in the Southwest throughout the "fun linen period." Simultaneously, the population of these states was also increasing. As a result, interest in household linen with southwestern themes increased.

When we think of the Southwest, it brings to mind cowboys, cacti, Pueblo villages, and American Indians. Most of these are represented in this chapter, which begins with cowboys and Indians and takes us back to the days before the Southwest was settled. The popularity of cowboy linen may well have been fueled by the entertainment industry. Cowboy and Indian films and television shows were very popular especially in the 1950s. Roy Rogers, Hopalong Cassidy, Gene Autry, John Wayne, and many more stars entertained the '50s audiences with their fictional adventures.

The next section of this chapter takes us to the deserts of the Southwest where we find cacti, birds, and donkeys. The birds and cacti placemat, napkin, and runner set (Item 13.10) in this section is the most collectible example in this chapter. We have only seen this set one other time. The set of donkey placemats and napkins (Item 13.8) is also very interesting. The donkey is seen in eight different poses. We have not been able to determine the correct sequence for the eight poses.

The final section of this chapter focuses on South American and Mexican household linen. This type of household linen became popular in America in the early 1940s and continued into the early years of the "fun linen period." Ties formed between the Mexican and American governments, and the popularity of Carmen Miranda may well have contributed to the popularity of this type of household linen.

The piece that brings South America to mind is the tablecloth (Item 13.11) with Carmen Miranda-type figures dancing around the border. Carmen Miranda was a famous singer and movie star in Brazil. She moved to America in 1940 where she resided until her death in 1955. In America she starred in various hit films and performed in nightclubs. Her trademark look was a hat with fruit and a wide, toothy grin. Some of her most famous films were *Springtime in the Rockies* and *Down Argentine Way*. The film *Springtime in the Rockies* inspired Americans to adopt her style of dress as a fad.

The household linen in the chapter with Mexican themes is currently gaining collectors' interest. The most unusual example is the laundry bag (Item 13.14). The most popular Mexican style collectibles are towels and tablecloths similar to Items 13.12 and 13.13.

Women's handkerchief designers did not often use Southwestern and South American themes. However, cowboys and Indians were quite popular in children's handkerchiefs. We have included two examples of cowboy motif children's handkerchiefs in this chapter (Items 13.5 and 13.15). The Charlie McCarthy Dude Cowboy handkerchief designed by Tom Lamb is probably the most collectible handkerchief example in this chapter.

13.2 Description: Texas Steers Towel, Tammis Keefe
Talk about well-dressed cuts of beef! This linen towel is one of our favorite Tammis Keefe towels. It is in mint condition with the original Belgian linen paper label. Each steer is wearing a different hat and has a prize ribbon with the name of a different cut of beef beside it. For an expensive dish like Chateau Briand, what could be more appropriate than a steer in a top hat? The Texas Longhorn in cowboy boots and wearing a ten-gallon hat would certainly raise some eyebrows back in Texas. Tammis Keefe also used this design for a tablecloth. A 1957 magazine ad featured the tablecloth: "It's round-up time at the barbecue pit, with the table wearing Tammis Keefe's hand printed linen cloth. Orange, brown and beige, 52 x 90 inches, [$]7.95; and napkins, .95. Matching apron, [$]3.95. Tumbler towel, [$]1.00. The Fashion Linens Shop, Lord & Taylor." Both the towel and the tablecloth are highly collectible. To date, we have not seen an example of either the napkins or the apron mentioned in the ad.
Measurements: 30"L x 16"W
Price Range:
$55-60 towel
$125-150 tablecloth

13.3 Description: Chuck Wagon Apron
This apron portrays the days of cooking in the wide-open spaces from the back of a covered wagon. This is a familiar scene from cowboy movies. The horse and the dog are enjoying the scene. The steak looks great! The back of the chuck wagon shows a kitchen complete with food, pots, and pans. This apron is faded and we consider it to be in poor condition.
Measurements: 30"L x 28"W
Price Range:
$22-25
$10-12 poor condition

13.4 Description: Western Saloon Towel
This mid-20th century towel has wonderful early 20th century details. There is so much to see that the eye doesn't know where to focus. Four colorfully dressed cowboys are ordering drinks at the bar with an advertisement for The Flora Dora Girls above their heads. The Flora Dora girls were the American equivalent of French cancan dancers in the early 20th century.
Measurements: 27.5"L x 16"W
Price Range: $40-45

13.5 Description: Western Handkerchief
This children's handkerchief was made for and sold at Neiman Marcus stores. It shows a boy and girl in Western outfits square dancing. The Neiman Marcus logo appears in the lower right corner.
Measurements: 13.5"L x 13.75"W
Price Range: $8-12

13.6 Description: Western Placemat, Towel, and Handkerchief, Pat Prichard
Pat Prichard created a series of items using this old western-inspired design. In addition to the three items pictured here, Ms. Prichard also used this pattern on dinnerware manufactured by Comstock. The linen placemat is one of a set of four. It has a machine-embroidered border. The linen towel has two of its original tags that read "Pure Linen" and "57 cents." All three items are easy to find.
Measurements:
12"L x 18.25"W, placemat
29"L x 17"W, towel
14.5" square, handkerchief
Price Range:
$28-32 set of four placemats
$20-25 towel
$12-15 handkerchief

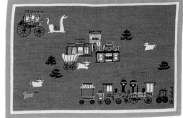

13.7 Description: American Indian Days of the Week Towels
There are seven towels, one for each day of the week. These towels were common in the pre-dishwasher days when dishes were dried by hand after washing. People actually used a different towel for each day of the week in those days. This set was painted and has not been used. There are very few sets of painted towels on the market. Very few sets were made and few of them have survived since the paint tended to deteriorate after repeated washings. There are numerous light brown marks on various towels in the set. We consider the set to be in poor condition. The second photograph shown here is a set of Aunt Martha's transfer patterns for the towels. The pattern says it was designed for towels but could be adapted for a child's quilt or curtains. It also says the pattern may be used for embroidered or painted towels.
Measurements: 32"L x 17"W
Price Range:
$50-60 set of seven
$15-20 set of seven, poor condition

13.8 Description: Donkey Placemat and Napkin Set
The set consists of eight embroidered placemats and napkins. There are eight different scenes of the donkey in different poses on the set. It seems the donkey is tied to a post then gains his freedom. While free, he sheds his baskets of fruit and smells the flowers. In another scene, he is tied to a post again. The embroidery work is good quality.
Measurements:
11"L x 17"W, placemat
16.5" square, napkin
Price Range: $75-100 sixteen-piece set

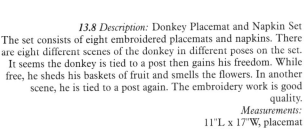

13.9 Description: Hand-Embroidered Runner
This runner has a man with a cart on one end and a woman with a cart on the other. The quality of the embroidery is good. It appears to be a home project. The edges of the runner are hand crochet.
Measurements: 38"L x 12.5"W
Price Range: $12-15

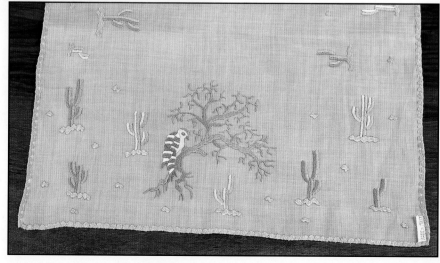

13.10 Description: Birds and Cacti Placemats, Napkins, and Runner
This hand-embroidered set of eight placemats, napkins, and a runner has its original label that reads "Made in Italy." Given this set's origins, the southwestern theme depicting various types of birds and cacti is rather unusual. If we had not acquired the tags with this set, we would have assumed it was made in Madeira. The workmanship and the organdy fabric are very high quality. One placemat, one napkin, and the runner are shown in the first photograph. The second photograph is a close-up of one end of the runner. This set is rare.
Measurements:
17"L x 16.25"W, napkins
16.5"L x 12"W, placemat
35"L x 17"W, runner
Price Range: $1,000-1,200 seventeen-piece set

13.11 *Description:* Carmen Miranda-Type Tablecloth
This tablecloth reminds us of Carmen Miranda. Women closely resembling
her are dancing around the border. The border also has various male figures
enjoying her dancing, playing instruments, and bringing her flowers. The
center has scattered fruit, urns, and flowers.
Measurements: 63"L x 44.5"W
Price Range: $75-100

13.12 Description: Carmen Miranda-Type Towel
It is a Carmen Miranda-type lady again! This example has much more detail than similar pieces of this era. The border is particularly interesting.
Collection of: Richard King
Measurements: 30"L x 15"W
Price Range: $25-30

13.13 Description: Mexican Theme Tablecloth
The border of this tablecloth shows three scenes from a Mexican town on each of its four sides. The cloth is very bright and the scenes are interesting. A second border has a row of colorful pottery. There are nine flower arrangements in rows near the center of the cloth.
Measurements: 53.5"L x 50.5"W
Price Range: $35-45

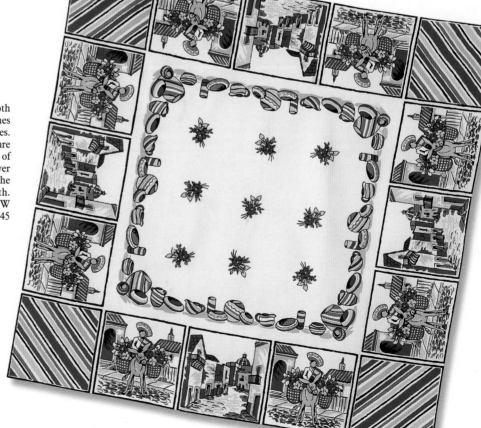

13.14 *Description:* Child's Laundry Bag
This laundry bag with a Mexican scene is very unusual. It is a home project. The male and female figures are done in cross-stitch and the embroidery is crude. It has been added to our collection because of its charm.
Measurements: 30.5"L x 15.5"W
Price Range: $25-30

13.15 *Description:* Charlie McCarthy Cowboy Handkerchief, Tom Lamb
This 1930s children's handkerchief by Tom Lamb is a fanciful portrayal of Charlie McCarthy, ventriloquist Edgar Bergen's famous dummy. The title *Charlie McCarthy, The Dude Cowboy* is printed underneath the image of Charlie on a bucking bronco. This handkerchief has one frayed corner and is slightly faded. It was also made in a red and blue version, an example of which sold for $120 at auction in February, 2002. We know of four Charlie McCarthy handkerchiefs made by Tom Lamb. All of them are rare. The other three titles in this series are *All American Drawback*, *At the Races*, and *Africa Speaks English*.
Measurements: 9.375"L x 9.5"W
Price Range:
$75-125
$25-45 poor condition

Sports are firmly rooted as a national pastime in America. Over the years different sports have won public favor. At the turn of the century, the average American enjoyed bicycle races, billiard matches, wrestling, baseball, and boxing. Upper-class Americans were engaged in tennis, golf, polo, fox hunting, horse racing, steeplechasing, and yachting.

It is interesting to note that unlike baseball, basketball and football were not among America's favorite spectator sports at the beginning of the century. Professional baseball teams were well established by the late 19th century and the first World Series was played in 1903. In contrast, basketball was not invented until 1891 and it took a considerable amount of time before it gained recognition. Although two minor professional basketball leagues existed before World War II, professional basketball in America under the aegis of the National Basketball Association (NBA) only began in 1950.

American football was also not invented until the late 19th century and it was initially held in low esteem with the American public because of the many casualties to players in the late 1800s. In fact, in 1905 the problem with football was so serious it prompted President Roosevelt to threaten to abolish the game if it was not made safer. Although professional football was played beginning in the late 19th century, the first American football league was not formed until the 1920s and the first National Football League (NFL) Super Bowl was not played until 1967. Household linen featuring baseball, basketball, and football is extremely rare. There are, however, numerous children's handkerchiefs featuring these sports. We have included an example of a football and a basketball handkerchief from the 1950s (Item 14.17) and a handkerchief depicting Donald Duck playing baseball (Item 14.11).

Amateur and professional sports competitions continued to be held during the Depression and World War II in America. Americans love sports and their continuance was important to the American spirit. In 1942 Commissioner Kenesaw Mountain Landis, who became professional baseball's first commissioner in 1920, wrote to President Franklin Roosevelt offering to discontinue the game for the duration of World War II and Roosevelt replied in a letter dated January 15, 1942, "I honestly feel it would be best for the country to keep baseball going."

When one considers the enduring popularity of sports in America, it is surprising to find that very few adult handkerchiefs or pieces of household linen with sports as the subject matter were made either before or during the "fun linen period." The majority of household linen with sports themes made prior to World War II feature horse racing, steeplechasing, fox hunting, or sailing themes. In terms of adult handkerchiefs, golf and tennis were the most popular sports themes both before and during the "fun linen period."

Although baseball, boxing, fishing, football, hunting, wrestling, basketball, bowling, tennis, and golf were the sports that commanded the most public interest during the "fun linen period," most of these popular sports did not evoke the interest of the textile designers of this period and they were rarely, if ever, represented on household linen and handkerchiefs. Despite the lack of popularity of these items, we have found a small number of interesting items for our collections and we included a number of pieces featuring bowling, fishing, hunting, tennis, and golf in this chapter. There are also a few examples of less popular sports such as water skiing in this chapter.

One possible explanation for the lack of sports related household linen is that very little entertaining revolved around most of the popular sports such as boxing, wrestling, basketball, and baseball games. Only four sports (fox hunting, horse racing, steeplechasing, and yachting) were routinely associated with parties and other events on the social calendar. Not surprisingly, these four sports are the ones most commonly found on fun household linen

Most of the items in this chapter feature people participating in various sports activities. Anthropomorphic themes are also included. One of Peggy's favorite examples is Item 14.3, the towel with the Scottish Terriers dressed in knickers playing golf. Scotland is the place where golf was invented so what could be more appropriate than a Scottish Terrier playing golf?

14.2 Description: Appliquéd Foxes Cocktail Napkins
Fox hunting has existed in North America since Colonial days and hunt balls are a long-standing tradition during hunting season. It is quite likely that the set of eight napkins pictured here was made for entertaining at a hunt-theme party. A fox, by itself, is unusual subject matter on cocktail napkins. Foxes are more typically found on tablecloths and towels in hunt scenes. These scenes usually include hounds and mounted hunters. The brown foxes on these napkins are hand sewn on white linen. Each fox is 2.75" tall. The scalloped borders are hand embroidered. The original paper labels are still glued to the backs of each napkin. The labels read "R N 14896, ALL LINEN, Embroidery all Cotton, Madeira Portugal." The quality of the embroidery is very good.
Measurements: 4.75"L x 8"W
Price Range: $65-75 set of eight

Opposite page: *14.1 Description:* Horse and Rider Cocktail Napkins
These hand-embroidered linen napkins with four different scenes tell the tale of a rider approaching a jump, going over, landing badly, and eventually falling off his horse. Most horse and rider designs depict the team jumping over a fence in fine style. Few depict such an embarrassing aftermath.
This set includes two napkins of each scene. There is a wealth of detail in this set including the interesting two-tone monogram, ALH.
Measurements: 5"L x 8"W
Price Range: $95-105 set of eight

14.3 Description: Golf, Golf, and More Golf
Scottish Terrier Golfers Towel: Two hand-embroidered Scottish Terriers dressed in traditional knickers are playing golf. This towel is yet another very interesting anthropomorphic theme. It retains its original paper label stating it is pure linen. The quality of the embroidery is somewhat crude; however, the unusual motif makes this piece appealing to collectors. This is the only towel we have seen with dogs playing golf.
Golf Ball Napkin: A hand-embroidered linen cocktail napkin showing a golf club about to hit a golf ball is seen at the bottom right of this picture. For something about to be whacked, this golf ball looks awfully cheerful. Surprisingly, in spite of the recent Tiger Woods-inspired surge in the popularity of golf, household linen with golf themes is not particularly popular with vintage household linen collectors at this time.
Appliquéd Golf Handkerchief: The appliquéd handkerchief retains its original paper label that reads "Gerbrend Creation, Handmade in Madeira, 60% cotton, 40% linen, exclusive of decoration."
Measurements:
9.75"L x 14.5"W, towel
7.5"L x 5"W, napkin
13.75"L x 14"W, handkerchief
Price Range:
$15-18 towel
$35-40 set of eight napkins
$12-14 handkerchief

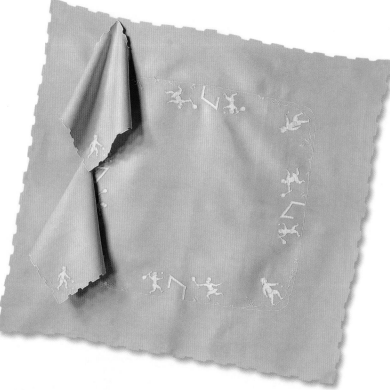

14.4 Description: Appliquéd Tennis Players Tablecloth and Napkins
The game of tennis originated in France in the 12th century where it was played in courtyards adjacent to castles or monasteries. In the earliest versions, the players hit the ball with their hands. Racquets were a later addition to the game. The appliquéd couple on this tablecloth is playing tennis in a modern setting with tennis racquets. The bar in the middle of the tablecloth represents a net. The figures are somewhat primitive and also lack one of the essentials for the 20th century version of the game, sneakers. The piece is entirely hand embroidered. Tennis motif tablecloths are unusual. There are four matching napkins.
Measurements:
34.25"L x 35"W, tablecloth
10.75"L x 11.5"W, each napkin
Price Range: $50-55 five-piece set

14.5 Description: Poodles in Hot Air Balloons Handkerchiefs, Pat Prichard
The sport of ballooning in North America dates to 1793. George Washington was present for the first flight in America, which was from Philadelphia to Gloucester County, New Jersey. Mr. Washington could never have visualized the black and hot pink poodles riding in very colorful hot air balloons on these handkerchiefs! The same design is pictured here in two color combinations. This is one of Pat Prichard's most popular handkerchief designs.
Measurements: 14.75"L x 15"W
Price Range: $25-30

14.6 *Description:* Appliquéd Steeplechase Tablecloth
Pictured here is a fabulous yellow linen tablecloth with appliquéd scenes of a steeplechase in the center of the cloth. Steeplechase derives its name from impromptu races by foxhunters in 18th century Ireland. This steeplechase tablecloth reminds us of the tailgate and corporate parties usually associated with steeplechase races in America today. Perhaps the original owner purchased it for entertaining at one of the many steeplechase events still being staged in America. The tablecloth is hand embroidered and the quality is uniformly excellent. The lovely soft colors of this tablecloth evoke the feelings often associated with a fine watercolor. The equine subject matter is very desirable. This tablecloth comes with twelve napkins.
Measurements: 110"L x 74"W
Price Range: $900-1,100 thirteen piece set

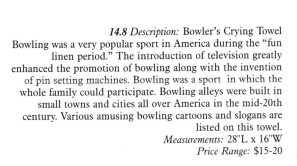

14.7 *Description:* Appliquéd Polo Player Placemat
Polo is not a sport commonly found on household linen although it is one of the world's oldest games, dating back to Ancient Persia. The sport was introduced in the United States in 1876. It has traditionally been associated with royalty and very wealthy people since it is an extremely expensive sport to pursue. This piece may have been a home project. The person who drew the appliqué patterns for the horse and rider was not a skilled illustrator. This horse is one of the most awkward animals we have ever seen. The piece is all hand embroidered and rather primitive. Its primitive design is part of its charm.
Measurements: 10.875"L x 17.75"W
Price Range: $7-8

14.8 *Description:* Bowler's Crying Towel
Bowling was a very popular sport in America during the "fun linen period." The introduction of television greatly enhanced the promotion of bowling along with the invention of pin setting machines. Bowling was a sport in which the whole family could participate. Bowling alleys were built in small towns and cities all over America in the mid-20th century. Various amusing bowling cartoons and slogans are listed on this towel.
Measurements: 28"L x 16"W
Price Range: $15-20

14.9 *Description:* Frustrated Lady Golfer, Sansome
This blonde beauty has a frustrated look on her face as her ball finds its way around instead of in the hole. Many of us are able to relate to this scene. This handkerchief is signed Sansome.
Measurements: 13"L x 12"W
Price Range: $25-30

14.10 *Description:* Appliquéd Lady Water-skiing Guest Towel
Water skiing is a relatively new sport. In 1922 a young American from Minnesota, Ralph Samuelson, proposed that if you could ski on snow you could ski on water. The lady on this towel is proving he was correct. She is gliding over the water in her bathing suit and rubber cap. Given the current fashion of thong bikinis, this lady looks positively overdressed!
Measurements: 21"L x 13.5"W
Price Range: $15-20

14.11 *Description:* Donald Duck Handkerchief
Disney cartoon characters and sports went hand in hand because they were both American favorites in the 20th century. In this scene Donald Duck is playing baseball, one of 20th century America's all time favorite sports. As he is pitching, his friends are cheering for him. "Copyright Walt Disney Productions" is printed on the bottom left of the handkerchief.
Measurements: 8.5"L x 9"W
Price Range: $12-15

14.12 *Description:* Harness Racing Tablecloth and Napkins

Harness racing is an American innovation dating back to the 19th century. This tablecloth is perfect for a picnic or party before the races. There is a driver on a sulky with his horse on each of the four sides of the cloth. Two horses' heads, the same size and design as those on the napkins, are placed toward the center of the tablecloth. The black horses' heads on the tablecloth and napkins are made from pieces of material, which are attached to the tablecloth with machine embroidery. The riders and the harnesses are machine embroidered. Each of the four napkins has a horse head on one corner. The edges of the cloth and the napkins are also machine embroidered.

Measurements:
45"L x 43.5"W, tablecloth
13.5" square, each napkin
Price Range: $50-60 five-piece set

14.13 *Description:* Charlie McCarthy At the Races Handkerchief, Tom Lamb

This is another handkerchief from Tom Lamb's Charlie McCarthy series. Charlie is shown at the racetrack ringing the starter's bell. Two corners are frayed and there is a large worn spot near one edge. This handkerchief is difficult to find and very collectible.
Measurements: 9.25"L x 9.5"W
Price Range:
$85-105
$40-60 poor condition

14.14 *Description:* Hunter's Crying Towel

This is a great "gag" gift for a hunter. There are lots of funny scenes on this towel. Our favorite scene is the one with the two hunters in the boat and the saying "Are all hunters liars? Or do all liars hunt?"
Measurements: 17"L x 23"W
Price Range: $15-20

14.15 Description: Fishing Handkerchief
This fishing theme handkerchief shows a fisherman, a leaping fish, and numerous fishing lures. The scalloped edge is machine embroidered.
Measurements: 11.75"L x 12"W
Price Range: $8-10

14.16 Description: Fishing Lures Cocktail Napkins
This set of eight linen cocktail napkins depicts eight different fishing lures. The napkins are shown in their original Leacock & Company, Inc. folder, copyright 1952. "Fine Irish Linen, Hand Printed-Hand Finished" is printed on the cover. The name of this set is "Trout Flies."
Measurements: 8.25"L x 5.25"W, each napkin
Price Range: $35-45 set of eight

14.17 Description: Basketball, Football, and Water Sports Handkerchiefs
The three 1950s handkerchiefs pictured here depict teenagers engaged
in various sports that were popular in America in the mid-20th century.
One handkerchief depicts various water sports such as sailing, surfing,
water skiing, diving, swimming, and canoeing. The children's basketball
handkerchief still has its original paper label that reads "A Burmel
Original, All Cotton." Note the old-fashioned footwear in the basketball
and football handkerchiefs. Clearly, they are pre-Nike!
Measurements:
13" square, water sports handkerchief
13" square, basketball handkerchief
13"L x 13.25"W, football handkerchief
Price Range: $12-15 each handkerchief

Chapter 15
Collecting 20th Century Fun Linen and Handkerchiefs

What to Collect: Two Golden Rules for Collecting

It is always difficult to give advice about collecting. Preferences for items change from time to time. Objects not considered collectible today might become very collectible in the future or vice versa. We are all familiar with collectibles that were actively pursued by collectors for a brief period of time and then lost their appeal almost overnight. A magazine or a newspaper article can affect the desirability of an item. A recent illustration of this point is discussed in Chapter 16. Vera towels recently experienced a sharp surge in popularity due to an article about collecting dishtowels in the June 2001 issue of Martha Stewart's magazine, *Living.*

The first golden rule for collecting is to purchase well-constructed items in good to mint condition that are made from high quality materials and exhibit interesting design. In general, this type of item is likely to be collected over a long span of time.

Designers' signatures or famous makers also enhance the collectibility of most items as long as the above conditions are met. The market for collectible hand-embroidered Madeira household linen is a good illustration of this point. Marghab was the most famous maker of Madeira household linen in the 20th century. Other firms also produced some extremely fine pieces. Unfortunately, none of their designs are as well documented as Marghab's designs; therefore, it is extremely difficult to determine the origin for even very fine pieces. Marghab items command a premium over other embroidered household linen made in Madeira because they are exceptional and well documented. We have seen some very fine non-Marghab examples sell at a discount partially because they could not be attributed to a famous manufacturer.

It should be noted that the rarity of an item does not necessarily directly correlate to its collectibility. A scarce item that is not appealing to a sufficient number of collectors may never appreciate in price. Rarity is more likely to have a positive effect on an item's price if the item meets the criteria for our *first golden rule of collecting.*

The second golden rule for collecting is to always remember there isn't anyone who can guarantee items will increase in value over time; therefore, it is best to buy things you admire. If a piece you truly admire never appreciates in value, it will not be a total loss if you have derived pleasure from owning it over the years.

Our own collections of fun household linen and handkerchiefs contain a very high percentage of signed items or pieces we can identify as having been designed by a particular maker. They also contain a large number of unusual and difficult to find items. In summary, we collect signed and rare pieces in most cases.

Aprons

Most aprons are not highly collectible at this time. There are a limited number of apron collectors and most 20th century aprons can be purchased for less than $20. However, there are exceptions and the very unusual designs or items signed by famous designers often command high prices. The Tony Sarg apron (Item 5.16) is a good example of a highly collectible apron. Another bar theme Tony Sarg apron sold for $202.50 at auction on April 6, 2002.

Black Americana

Household linen depicting black Americans has become very popular. Although many items were produced, there are a significant number of collectors and prices are rising. Printed tablecloths seem to command the highest prices. We recorded numerous sales in the price range of $150-$300 in the past two years. Towels are also popular collectibles. Prices for towels range from $5-$85.

Chenille Bedspreads

Adult and children's chenille bedspreads have fallen in and out of fashion since their "heyday" in the 1950s. They are currently very desirable. The most collectible adult bedspreads have peacock designs. Both single and double peacock designs are still easy to find. Children's bedspreads usually had fairy tales, cowboys, or cowgirls as subject matter. Bedspreads with Cinderella and Roy Rogers as the theme are particularly popular. Occasionally, children's bedspreads were made with matching curtains. The curtains are rare and sets consisting of bedspreads with matching curtains often sell for over $200. The buyer should be cautious when seeking to purchase vintage chenille bedspreads since some of the old designs are being reproduced today.

Cocktail Napkins

Cocktail napkins are very popular with collectors of fun linen. There are a very large number of interesting napkin designs on the market and collectors can easily build impressive fun linen collections with cocktail napkins alone. They are especially representative of 20th century fun household linen because they did not exist prior to the 20th century.

Cocktail napkins were often sold in decorative boxes or folders and given as presents. To this day, we often find cocktail napkins in unused condition still in their original packaging. We have included an example of a set of Georges Briard napkins in their original, very distinctive, pink and black gift box in Chapter 7 (Item 7.6) and examples of napkins in their original cardboard folders in various chapters. Tammis Keefe took a slightly different approach and designed some gift boxes to match specific cocktail napkin designs. Leacock & Company, Inc., Dervan, and Fodor were the most famous manufacturers of napkins in folders. Of the three, Leacock was the most prolific manufacturer. The Fodor folders were made of a much softer cardboard than those made by Leacock & Company, Inc. Most of the Fodor folders we have observed are in fragile condition, which may be the reason they are so difficult to find.

The vast majority of cocktail napkins were unsigned; however, Georges Briard, Depler, Tammis Keefe, Tom Lamb, Tony Sarg, Carl Tait, Vera, Paul Webb, and Virginia Zito are all known to have signed cocktail napkins. Signed cocktail napkins command a premium in the current market. Figural shaped napkins, like those pictured in Items 1.6 and 5.10, and napkins with people (particularly naughty ladies) or animal motifs are very popular today and they also sell at a premium versus the average unsigned set. The price range for most non-figural sets of eight napkins is $25-$45. However, figural sets like the horse and pig shaped napkins (Item 1.6) often sell for $100-$150. In general, sets of eight to twelve napkins are highly desirable. Sets of five or less are often purchased for less than $15 unless the subject matter is very interesting or unusual. The set of four art deco ladies cocktail napkins pictured as Item 5.25 is an example of a set of four napkins, which would command a premium price.

Placemats

Placemats are not particularly collectible at this time. The vast majority were not signed. The subject matter for placemats varies to include most of the topics covered in this book. We have included printed, embroidered, and lace placemats in the chapters featuring birds, the circus, cocktails, flowers, food, naughty, southwest, and sports. Vera, Tammis Keefe, Faith Austin, Pat Prichard, and Tony Sarg are all known to have signed placemats.

Printed Handkerchiefs

Handkerchiefs have always been a popular collectible. Until recently, however, handkerchiefs produced in the early 20th century were far more collectible than handkerchiefs produced during the "fun linen period." Today many unsigned and designer handkerchiefs by artists who were famous as well as obscure during this period are collectible. The designer, anthropomorphic, figural, humorous motif, and unusual flower-shaped handkerchiefs tend to command higher prices than the unsigned, traditional floral examples in most cases. This may be true in part because unsigned, traditional floral handkerchiefs were more popular and less expensive during this period and they were produced in much larger quantities than the other types of handkerchiefs.

Some of the most humorous unsigned items were the "How to" handkerchiefs that were popular in the 20th century. There are amusing "How to" handkerchiefs on a variety of subjects such as how to speak various foreign languages, how to cure insomnia, and so forth. They even made "How to Get a Husband" and "How to Keep Your Husband" handkerchiefs, and we have included examples in Chapter 12 (Item 12.6). We also have an example of a "How to Cure a Hangover" handkerchief (Item 5.23). "How to" handkerchiefs are currently very popular with collectors. The "How to Get a Husband" and "How to Keep Your Husband" handkerchiefs pictured in Chapter 12 currently sell in the price range of $50-$65.

Some of the signatures we have found on printed handkerchiefs are: Brigitta Ajnefors, Betty Anderson, Kit Ann, Mabel Lucie Atwell, Faith Austin, Ivan Bartlett, Mary Blair, Bonheur, Ceil Chapman, Henry Charles, Collette, Jo Copeland, Don, Eric Fisher, Thomas Fisher, Frederique, Jean Hannau, Peter Hunt, Kati, Tammis Keefe, Lori King, Billie Kompa, Tom Lamb, Mary Lewis, Liliane, Marielle, Ann McCann, Dwaine Meek, Jeanne Miller, Monique, Erin O'Dell, Pat Prichard, Rachelle, Rutherford, Tony Sarg, Ann Samstag, Sansome, Carol Schnurer, Carol Stanley, Carl Tait, Peg Thomas, Vera, Sally Victor, Hazel Ware, Phila Webb, Welcher, Emily Whaley, Wilcke, and Virginia Zito. The best Tammis Keefe, Carl Tait, Tom Lamb, and Mary Blair handkerchiefs are currently the most desirable in today's marketplace.

Children's handkerchiefs are also popular collectibles. For readers who have a particular interest in this type of handkerchief, we recommend one of our favorite books on this subject by J.J. Murphy titled *Children's Handkerchiefs, A Two Hundred Year History*. In terms of children's handkerchiefs, handkerchief books are the most desirable collectibles. Children's handkerchief books were quite expensive at the time they were made. Consequently, limited quantities were sold especially when compared to the vast quantities of children's handkerchiefs sold throughout the 20th century. Few complete handkerchief books have survived and they are very difficult to find in good condition.

The most prolific sources of printed handkerchiefs were Burmel, Carol Stanley, Disney, Franshaw, Hamilton, Herrmann Handkerchief Company of New York, J. H. Kimball & Company, Inc., Lady Heritage, and Robinson and Golluber, Inc. There are handkerchiefs signed by Carol Stanley as well as handkerchiefs bearing other signatures with paper labels stating that they were from the studio of Carol Stanley. For instance, Mary Blair is known to have designed handkerchiefs for the studio of Carol Stanley.

Handkerchiefs were sold at specialty counters in major department stores throughout the United States. We have found tags or original packaging from Bonwit Teller, J.C. Penney Co., Lord & Taylor, Marshall Field, Neiman Marcus, and Saks Fifth

Avenue to name a few. The signed handkerchiefs were expensive during the height of their popularity in the 1950s and the '60s. Original price tags from Lord & Taylor indicate that some of these handkerchiefs were sold for as much as $1, which would amount to over $6 today.

Printed Tablecloths

Printed tablecloths are experiencing a surge in popularity and prices have been rising accordingly. Printed tablecloths were made with all types of subject matter and they are included in almost every chapter of this text. Both signed and unsigned tablecloths are popular collectibles. The vast majority of printed tablecloths are unsigned. To date, we have observed tablecloths signed by Ivan Bartlett, Tammis Keefe, Pat Prichard, Tony Sarg, Carl Tait, Luther Travis, Vera, and Virginia Zito. In terms of the signed tablecloths available in the marketplace, Vera items are the most plentiful. Tony Sarg tablecloths typically sell for well over $100. Some Tammis Keefe and Vera linen tablecloths regularly command prices of $75 and up. Other less popular Tammis Keefe and Vera tablecloths sell for between $15 and $65. Most of the tablecloths signed by other designers sell in the same $35 to $65 price range as the better unsigned tablecloths. The more common unsigned cotton tablecloths with floral motifs can be found for as little as $5.

In terms of manufacturers, we have found examples bearing the labels of Broderie Creations, California Hand Prints, Dervan, Fabrés, Falfax, Floembco, Fodor, Hardy Craft, Leacock & Company, Inc., Paragon Needlecrafts, Simtex, Startex, and Wilendur.

Towels

Towels, especially printed examples, are extremely popular today. This is partially true because there were so many fabulous 20th century designs and also because towels can be used in so many different ways. Some collectors are using them to make cushions or as table runners. Other collectors are framing them. Many of the 20th century kitchen towels are very striking and make wonderful wall hangings. In a similar fashion to tablecloths, the vast majority of towels are unsigned. To date, we have seen printed towels signed by Faith Austin, Ivan Bartlett, Georges Briard, Francis Dearden, Depler, Don, Suzie Doria, Kati, Tammis Keefe, Tom Lamb, Lois Long, C.P. Meier, Pat Prichard, Mary Sarg, Tony Sarg, Carl Tait, Peg Thomas, Luther Travis, Vera, Don Wight, George Wright, and Virginia Zito.

In terms of manufacturers, we have found examples with labels from Fabrés, Falfax, Fallani and Cohn, Leacock & Company, Inc., Parisian Prints, Simtex, Startex, and Townhouse Originals.

Signed printed towels often command a premium over comparable quality unsigned examples. A Vera floral-theme towel similar to Item 7.9 would sell for at least double the price of a comparable unsigned example.

The most desirable unsigned examples have an unusual or very striking design, feature a popular motif such as dogs, or

depict well-known pop culture figures. A printed towel of Blondie and Dagwood with a 1950 copyright recently sold at auction for $103.50.

Embroidered towels from transfer patterns were popular 20th century home craft projects. The designs for the towels were sold as hot transfer patterns, which could be ironed onto towels then embroidered or painted. The patterns had recommended colors of thread printed on the instructions. Aunt Martha's, McCalls, and Vogart produced many of the most popular patterns. Seven days of the week and his and hers motifs were the best selling motifs. Scenes on the seven days of the week towels portrayed people, animals, or reptiles doing different chores for each day of the week or often, in the case of animals, being mischievous. If the subject matter was chores, the Sunday towel typically showed a day of rest or a scene with a church.

Vintage seven days of the week towel sets are popular with collectors. Complete sets are difficult to find and prices are rising. However, sets made in the last quarter of the 20th century are plentiful and inexpensive. Many of the sets available on the market today are reproductions made from old patterns or from reprints of the old patterns, some of which are still available from Aunt Martha's in Kansas City, Missouri. In addition, ready-made sets are available today in mail-order catalogues. We saw a set with sunbonnet girls made in India advertised in a recent Lillian Vernon catalogue for $24.98. These later reproductions do not command the same prices as the original pieces. Original vintage sets currently sell for a minimum of $50. Single towels with all seven days printed on one towel were also produced. They are more difficult to find but are not as popular as the seven towel sets.

Other collectible embroidered towels include his and hers, naughty, and anthropomorphic designs as the subject matter. Paragon Needlecraft and Floembco produced many of the naughty lady towels seen in Chapter 11.

Where to Buy

We are often asked about where we find items for our collections. We purchase items from many different sources: antique shops, antique shows, flea markets, estate sales, garage sales, private collections, and auctions. It is important to study household linen and handkerchief prices before you enter the market as a buyer. We also recommend that you carefully review our definitions for condition (see Introduction, page 9) and use them as a guide. This is especially important if you wish to acquire a collection, which will appreciate in value over the years. There are many sources for household linen and handkerchiefs and you will not find any source that will always be cheaper than the others. We have made some wonderful buys at unexpected places over the years.

We cannot place enough emphasis on the importance of inspecting an item before you make a purchase. Depending on the terms of sale, it can be difficult, if not impossible, to obtain a refund after you have purchased the item. Inaccurate representations by sellers are not necessarily intentional. It is important to remember that other people's definitions of excellent condition are not necessarily the same as yours. The phrase "in great condition for its age" probably causes the most confusion between buyers and sellers. Sellers who do not normally deal in vintage textiles often believe that textiles could not survive fifty or sixty years without showing signs of wear. We have seen items described in this manner that upon closer inspection turn out to have condition problems such as fading, holes, tears, stains, or frayed edges or corners.

The chances of a misunderstanding between buyer and seller are even greater in cases where you are buying solely on the basis of a photograph(s) and a written description. Buyers would do well to remember the old adage: *caveat emptor* (let the buyer beware) especially when buying an item that they are not physically able to view before purchase.

Market Conditions

A confluence of events in late 20th century America combined to escalate the prices of collectible 20th century fun household linen and handkerchiefs. Sustained economic growth over an unprecedented number of years during the Clinton presidency led to sky-high consumer confidence, higher disposable incomes, and strong consumer spending throughout much of the 1990s. At the same time, a number of museum exhibitions increased awareness of a group of very talented 20th century textile designers, giving their work a much wider audience and newfound respectability. Technological advances in the form of the Internet and on-line auctions such as eBay ensure wide distribution: 24 hours a day, seven days of the week, from the comforts of home or the office. Baby boomers with very comfortable incomes indulged their feelings of nostalgia and recaptured their childhoods with purchases of collectible toys, books, household linen, and other items "just like" things they had when they were growing up.

From a practical standpoint, 20th century household linen and handkerchiefs also appeal to collectors on multiple levels. Although prices are rising, they are still relatively inexpensive especially when compared to items such as collectible toys and dolls from the same period. In addition, linens are very versatile and they can be used in the home as they were originally intended or as decorations in the form of wall hangings, cushion covers, and so forth. Handkerchiefs are also interesting when framed. In addition, they have been incorporated into quilts to create wonderful visual effects. Most pieces of household linen and handkerchiefs are durable and easy to maintain. For all the above reasons, 20th century fun household linen and handkerchiefs are gaining in popularity among collectors and we expect this trend to continue for some time to come.

Chapter 16

20th Century Fun Linen Designers

When we decided to include a chapter about textile designers in this text, we realized it would be a difficult task. Although colleges and universities world-wide provide instruction in textile design and have significant library holdings on the subject of textile design, very little information on the designers of 20th century household linen and handkerchiefs is available. Unlike fashion designers, even the most successful textile designers often remain anonymous for their entire careers. A great deal of the information we have been able to collect for this text was available because the textile artist was also a distinguished painter, illustrator, or as in the case of Georges Briard, a famous designer of household products.

Ivan Bartlett (1908-1976)

Ivan Bartlett was born in Plainfield, Vermont on February 3, 1908. He was a student at the prestigious Chouinard School of Art in Los Angeles. He is best known as a lithographer, illustrator, engraver, muralist, and painter and is listed in *Who Was Who in American Art*. He was a resident of Long Beach, California in the 1930s and was very active in the California art community in the 1930s and '40s. Various exhibitions of his fine art were held in California during this period. He also worked as a textile and wallpaper designer in the 1940s. He subsequently moved to New York City where he was active as an artist through the 1960s. We have included an example of his best-known tablecloth, a cowboy design, in Chapter 13 (Item 13.1). He also designed handkerchiefs and towels. All of his textile designs are difficult to find.

Mary Blair (1911-1978)

Mary Browne Robinson (Mary Blair) was born on October 21, 1911, in McAlester, Oklahoma. She met her future husband, Lee Everett Blair, a fellow student at the prestigious Chouinard School of Art in Los Angeles, in 1931 and the couple wed on March 3, 1934.

Mary Blair was one of the most successful and prominent American female commercial artists in the mid-20th century. She was extremely versatile and was involved in the design of an eclectic mix of items ranging from textiles to animated films to name a few. Examples of her textiles are extremely rare. To the best of our knowledge, the few items she designed for Disney hotels are the only examples of her household textile designs. She also designed several handkerchief designs for Carol Stanley in the 1950s. Some of these designs were featured in magazine ads for Lord & Taylor. Mary Blair handkerchiefs sold at retail for as much as $1 in the 1950s. An example of one of her handkerchiefs is pictured as Item 1.19. Her handkerchiefs are highly collectible and typically sell in a range between $65 and $125.

The Disney studio hired Mary in 1940 and Disney employed her until 1953. Her art can be seen in many well-known short and full-length animated films such as *The Three Caballeros*, *The Little House*, *Song of the South*, *Cinderella*, *So Dear to My Heart*, *Melody Time*, *Alice In Wonderland*, and *Peter Pan*.

Mary was extremely productive as a commercial artist in the 1950s and '60s. She illustrated children's books (such as *Baby's House* and *I Can Fly*) and advertisements (Pall Mall cigarettes, Johnson baby products, Nabisco, and Pepsodent among others) and produced designs for American Artists greeting cards. She also designed sets for Christmas and Easter shows at Radio City Music Hall in New York City.

A decade after she left Disney, she returned to work for the studio when Walt Disney asked her to design the dolls for the *It's A Small World* attraction for the 1964 World's Fair held in New York. The attraction was a huge success at the World's Fair and was subsequently moved to Disneyland in California and then duplicated in the other Disney theme parks that have opened. Other Mary Blair projects for Disney included a mural, a carpet pattern, and forty pieces of furniture for the Polynesian Hotel.

Georges Briard

Georges Briard, whose real name was Jascha Brojdo, was an artist and a designer. He was born in the Russian Ukraine and his family moved to Poland when he was four. He migrated to America in 1937 and earned a Master of Fine Arts degree from a joint program offered by the University of Chicago and the Art Institute of Chicago.

He was a prolific designer of household linen and objects, barware, hostess accessories, and small furnishings during the "fun linen period." In the 1950s designers did not usually lend their names to products and when they did their name was noted on the back of the product with the company logo. In a departure from this practice, Jascha's products were sold with his pseudonym, Georges Briard, prominently displayed on the front of the items. His designs were affordable and accessible to middle-class Americans and they found their way into a large number of American households. Housewives in the 1950s were thrilled to receive gifts designed by Georges Briard and his items were very popular as shower and wedding gifts.

In terms of household linen, Georges Briard designed cocktail napkins, towels, and aprons to complement his house wares line. His cocktail napkins were sold in sets of eight in decorative boxes, similar to the one pictured in Item 7.6. These sets are relatively easy to find and are perennial favorites with fun household linen collectors. Aside from the flowers pictured in Item 7.6, other motifs we have seen on Briard napkins cover a wide range of subject matter such as butterflies, bees, hot air balloons, chess pieces, angels, and wine bottles. His towels and aprons are much more difficult to find; however, they are not as collectible as his napkins.

One of Georges Briard's innovations in the giftware market was to design a line of gift-boxed products, which allowed the shopper to purchase a moderately priced gift set in one package. One of his most popular gift sets included two poodle hand towels and two matching glasses for the bathroom. The towels from one of his poodle-theme sets are pictured as Item 10.8.

Constance Depler

Based on copyright dates on some of her designs, we know that Constance Depler was active as an illustrator of prints and designer of household items and linen in the 1950s. To date, all the examples we have seen of her work depict various animals, particularly dogs, in anthropomorphic poses. In terms of household linen, she designed cocktail napkins and towels. Leacock & Company, Inc. produced her cocktail napkins. They were sold in sets of eight in decorative presentation folders. Two very typical examples of her whimsical cocktail napkin sets are pictured as Items 3.1 and 5.9 in this text. She used only her last name, Depler, when signing household linen. However, she used her full name when signing paper napkin sets and prints. Her paper napkin designs were also sold in decorative gift boxes. Examples of her household linen designs are difficult to find and her cocktail napkins are currently quite popular with collectors.

Tammis Keefe (1920-1960)

Margaret Thomas Keefe was born in California in 1920. Her delightful whimsical handkerchiefs signed with her pseudonym, Tammis Keefe, are well known to collectors of 20th century handkerchiefs. Examples of her textile designs have been featured in various exhibits in the second half of the 20th century. One of the earliest was held in 1956 at The Philadelphia Museum of Art. The exhibit included 101 of her handkerchiefs. One of the most recent exhibits to include examples of her work was held at the Fashion Institute of Technology's museum (The Museum at FIT) in New York City from October 17, 2000 to January 13, 2001. The exhibit was titled *A Woman's Hand: Designing Textiles in America, 1945 – 1969.* The exhibit was co-curated by Lynn Felsher, Curator of Textiles, and Joanne Dolan, Associate Curator of Textiles, at the museum. The cover of the exhibit's brochure pictured Keefe's "Lemons", a screen-printed cotton and rayon furnishing fabric made by Golding Decorative Fabrics in 1949. This fabric was also shown in the MOMA *Good Design* exhibition of 1950.

Phoebe Ann Erb's article in the April/May 2000 issue of the *American Craft* magazine mentions that Tammis Keefe designed handkerchiefs under the pseudonym Peg Thomas. We have also seen examples bearing the signature P. Thomas. Considerably fewer handkerchiefs were produced using the Peg Thomas or P. Thomas signature. Consequently, they are more difficult to find than examples signed Tammis Keefe. Even though they are more difficult to find at this time, the most interesting Peg Thomas handkerchiefs sell for much lower prices than the most collectible handkerchiefs with the Tammis Keefe signature. Peg Thomas handkerchiefs typically sell for $20 and up. Ms. Keefe also designed kitchen towels with the Peg Thomas signature. Examples of towels with this signature are scarce.

Tammis Keefe handkerchiefs were produced and marketed by J.H. Kimball & Company (Kimball) between 1947 and 1958. Many Tammis Keefe handkerchiefs can be found in unused condition with their original distinctive yellow and gold Kimball paper labels still attached. We have also found a few handkerchiefs with a Hamilton yellow and gold paper label.

Tammis Keefe produced most handkerchief designs in several different color combinations. Prices for the same design may vary with the color. For instance, the series of handkerchiefs she designed with Santa cavorting with his reindeer (Item 3.11) are usually found in traditional red and green. However, two other versions were made with light blue and white and pink and white backgrounds. Even though the blue and pink versions are much more difficult to find, the more traditional red and green version is very collectible and commands a higher price.

It is not difficult to build a collection of Tammis Keefe handkerchiefs. She was the most prolific designer of ladies handkerchiefs in the 20th century. It is not clear how many handkerchiefs she designed in her brief career. At least one account reports over four hundred designs. This number is astonishing considering the wide range of designs she produced and the quality of her work. To the best of our knowledge, Ms. Keefe did not have other designers producing designs under her name.

Some Tammis Keefe designs are more collectible than others. Her whimsical, almost cartoon style handkerchiefs are the most popular. Her figural designs and examples from her famous places and cities series are currently the most desirable to collectors. Her designs with geometric patterns or simple floral designs are not currently popular and typically sell for between $5 and $15. Many of her most popular designs regularly sell for $30 and up. Over the past two years, we have seen record prices for several Tammis Keefe handkerchiefs at auctions. The most expensive handkerchiefs are from her famous places and cities series. Palm Springs with its original Kimball yellow and gold paper label sold for $91 at auction in the summer of 2000. Olvera St. Los Angeles (without its original Kimball paper label) sold for $102.50 at approximately the same time. In August 2000, Tammis Keefe's Grand Central Terminal, New York City handkerchief, with its original Kimball label, sold for $103.50 at auction. A few days after this, a record price of $203.50 was paid at auction for her Laguna Beach, California handkerchief. This handkerchief also had its original Kimball label.

As a textile designer, Tammis Keefe is best known for her handkerchief designs; however, she also designed scarves (in cotton, silk, and synthetic fabrics), tablecloths, placemat and napkin sets, cocktail napkins, runners, towels, aprons, furnishing fabrics, and menswear fabrics. She began designing scarves for Kimball in 1953. She was the second American woman to sign her name to scarves. Vera was the first.

Most of the Tammis Keefe table linen that we have seen to date is made of linen fabric. Her table linen was expensive. An ad in a 1955 magazine listed her 72" round tablecloth titled *Ice Cream Social Cloth* at $11.95. The matching 17" square napkins originally retailed for $0.89 cents each. Unsigned linen tablecloths of comparable size retailed for less than $5 at that time. Most of her tablecloths currently range in price from $45 to $85. An example would be the tablecloth pictured as Item 7.5. A few designs regularly sell for over $100. The tablecloth pictured as Item 8.4 is an example from this latter category.

Ms. Keefe's cocktail napkins are all highly collectible and sets of eight in the most popular designs regularly sell for $50 and up. She also designed gift boxes to match some of her cocktail napkin designs. These gift boxes are difficult to find; however, they are not particularly popular with Tammis Keefe collectors at this time.

Tammis Keefe towels are also highly collectible. Many Tammis Keefe as well as kitchen towel collectors use the towels as runners or wall hangings. Tammis Keefe towels currently range in price from $5 to $65. In terms of non-textile items, Tammis Keefe also designed playing cards, greeting cards, pottery, and at least one game that we have seen. A 1959 ad mentions a Tammis Keefe Fortune-teller towel that retailed for $1 at Lord & Taylor and Marshall Field. This towel had a matching Fortune Card game, which was also designed by Tammis Keefe. It sold at retail for $3.50.

Textile companies that used Tammis Keefe's designs include: Golding Decorative Fabrics, Fallani and Cohn, Goodall Fabrics, and Marlboro Shirt Company.

Tom Lamb (1896-1988)

Thomas Babbitt Lamb, known to collectors as Tom Lamb, was born in 1896. According to J.J. Murphy, author of *Children's Handkerchiefs, A Two Hundred Year History*, "Tom Lamb designed more handkerchiefs than any other modern illustrator who signed his or her work." He studied at the Art Students League and New York University and began his career as a cartoonist, illustrator, and writer of children's books. In the early 1920s he had a monthly page for children called *Kiddyland Movies* in *Good Housekeeping* magazine. This popular page resulted in a line of Kiddyland products such as talcum powder and hand-

kerchiefs. During the 1920s, '30s, and '40s Tom Lamb became one of the best-known designers of children's handkerchiefs. In the 1940s he made a successful transition to a new career as an industrial designer and inventor. His numerous inventions included a lounge chair, piggy banks, and even rifles for the U.S. army in World War II. His designs for handles for kitchen utensils, cutlery, surgical instruments, and other tools were the subject of a one-man show at the Museum of Modern Art in 1948.

Tom Lamb's early handkerchiefs are signed with his initials, while later designs have his full signature. In addition to the Dionne series pictured in Chapter 12 (Item 12.23), Tom Lamb was commissioned by various other firms to design several other handkerchief series based on famous figures. He designed at least four handkerchiefs for a Charlie McCarthy set. Two handkerchiefs from this series are pictured as Item 13.15 and Item 14.14. He also designed four Smokey the Bear handkerchiefs for the United States Forest Service. The more common examples of Tom Lamb's handkerchiefs typically sell for $5 to $25. One of his more difficult to find designs, the Charlie McCarthy *Africa Speaks English* handkerchief, recently sold for over $100 at auction. Handkerchiefs from his Smokey the Bear series usually sell for $40 to $60.

Tom Lamb also designed towels and cocktail napkins. His napkin sets usually came in cardboard presentation folders with his name prominently displayed on the covers. Examples of both his towels and his napkins are difficult to find. An example of one of his towel designs is pictured as Item 8.32. His towels usually sell for $25 and up. His napkin sets typically sell for between $25 and $50.

Vera Way Marghab (1900-1995)

Vera and her husband, Emile Marghab, founded Emile Marghab Inc., New York, and Marghab, Ltd., Madeira in 1934. The business sold fine household linen in shops in New York, Los Angeles, Dallas, and Minneapolis in the United States, and Melbourne and Sydney in Australia. The household linen was primarily designed by Vera and manufactured in Madeira, Portugal. After Emile's death in 1947, Vera managed the business on her own until 1984 when the political situation in Madeira forced her to close. During the fifty years that Marghab linens were produced, Vera introduced over three hundred different designs. A marvelous and very extensive collection of her designs is on display at the South Dakota Art Museum in Brookings, South Dakota. This museum also published a book on Vera Marghab in 1998 titled *Perfection, Never Less: The Vera Way Marghab Story* by D. J. Cline. This book is an excellent reference for all collectors of Marghab and can be purchased directly from the museum.

In terms of collectible 20th century Madeira household linen, Marghab items are some of the most collectible and most expensive. Many Marghab placemats, tablecloths, and runners were made with Margandie, an extremely fine organdy fabric made by the Fischbacher Company in Switzerland. Napkins and towels were typically made with a slightly heavier linen fabric.

Many of the Marghab linens found today do not have cloth or paper labels attached to them. In these cases, the best method of identification is to consult the list of Marghab designs in the book mentioned above. Some designs are more desirable and more expensive than others. Marghab household linen with the original labels and pieces without any identifying labels or tags command the same prices. Condition is the important factor in determining price.

Two of the most expensive designs are "Delphinium" (Item 7.1) and "Deer". Prices for "Deer" pieces are comparable to those for "Delphinium". Tablecloths large enough for at least eight place settings with matching napkins in the more elaborate patterns like "Hortensia" can sell for well over $1,000.

It should be noted that companies other than Marghab also produced wonderful embroidered household linen in Madeira in the 20th century and Madeira continues to be an important source of embroidered household linen in the 21st century. However, not all embroidery produced in Madeira in the 20th century was of fine quality. A considerable amount of mediocre merchandise was also produced. There is an unfortunate tendency in today's collectible linen market to attribute mediocre embroidery to China. Any household linen thought to originate in China is severely discounted. Conversely, mediocre items known to be made in Madeira are often priced outrageously simply because they were made in Madeira. This practice makes very little sense to us. Price should be closely linked to the quality of the workmanship and design of a specific piece and not solely to its maker or the place where it was made.

Having said this, we should point out that we know of at least one Marghab design that was copied by Chinese manufacturers. As discussed in the caption for Item 12.12, although the color of the thread is almost identical, the quality of the linen fabric is very different. The material used in the Chinese example is considerably coarser and there is a significant difference in price between the two sets of napkins. In this particular case, there is a clear difference in quality, which justifies the difference in price between the Marghab napkins and the napkins made in China.

Jeanne Miller

We have documented Jeanne Miller's designs from the 1960s by locating several examples of her work with 1965 copyrights. To date, we have been unable to find examples of her work dated either before or after the 1960s. All of the dated examples we have located had fabric labels stating they were by a. Skandia Prints, Robinson and Golluber, Inc. We have also found undated signed handkerchiefs with the distinctive yellow and gold J. H. Kimball & Company, Inc. paper labels. Therefore, we know she worked with at least two handkerchief manufacturers. We have also encountered Jeanne Miller's signature on scarves.

Jeanne Miller handkerchiefs are relatively easy to find. A few handkerchiefs, such as the one promoting the Democratic Party (Item 1.27) and the companion Republican Party piece, have a value of $20 or more. However, the vast majority of her handkerchiefs sell for less than $20. Her designs are not currently as popular as those of Mary Blair, Tammis Keefe, Pat Prichard, or Carl Tait.

Vera Neumann (1907-1993)

Vera Neumann (Vera) was a painter as well as a famous textile designer. She studied at Cooper Union and Traphagen School of Fashion. Cooper Union awarded her the Outstanding Alumna Award. Her paintings were exhibited in many countries. She traveled widely in Europe and the Orient and her work was influenced by her interest in primitive art forms, crafts, and nature. Early in her career she designed children's furniture and murals.

In 1946, Vera and George Neumann and F. Werner Hamm, a textile expert, each contributed $1,000 to start a business. Vera's first design was a placemat. The company's first order was from B. Altman and Company for three placemats made from parachute silk. When Vera attended an exhibit of her work at the Goldie Paley Design Center at Philadelphia University, she told the curators that the only thing small enough to print was a placemat since all their silk screening was done on her kitchen table.

A press release from 1973 issued by the New York public relations firm, Rea Luber, Inc., mentions that Vera added her trademark ladybug to her signature on this first placemat because she thought her name alone looked too bare. She chose ladybugs because she loved the way they looked and knew they were a symbol of good luck in many parts of the world. The ladybug was eventually dropped from her signature in her later pieces.

Vera became a prolific designer of scarves. She designed her first scarf in 1947. Her signature scarves were the first "designer scarves" created by an American woman. Her style included bold geometric, folk art, stylized floral, and abstract designs. One of her companies, Scarves by Vera, had showrooms on Fifth Avenue and she continued to supply designs for the company until several months before her death.

Vera was also a prolific designer of household linen: tablecloths, placemats, napkins, cocktail napkins, kitchen towels, hostess aprons, potholders, toaster covers, sheets, pillowcases, blankets, bedspreads, draperies, and bath towels. She also designed other items for the home: shower curtains, bath accessories for Burlington, and stoneware for Mikasa. In addition, she produced various lines of clothing including shirts, blouses, shifts, dresses, pants, and lingerie. Vera designs typically incorporated bright colors in strong combinations, often with her favorite color, orange. Vera was a master of designing products for the mass market, a new phenomenon in America. An Associated Press release in 1977 reported, "Vera designs were sold in over 1,200 stores with sales of more than $100 million."

Vintage Vera household linen is readily available today and many examples of her work can still be found in their original packaging. Her towels are currently very popular with collectors. They experienced a sharp surge in popularity in the summer of 2001 and many of the prices doubled. This occurred after they were featured in an article about collecting dishtowels in the June 2001 issue of Martha Stewart's magazine, *Living*. Her other household linen, such as tablecloths and placemats, is less in demand and can still be purchased very reasonably. To illustrate the rather large disparity in prices, many Vera floral or fruit-theme towels are selling for $30 to $40 while tablecloths with similar themes can still be purchased for $20 or less.

Vera was a member of the Board of Directors of the American Crafts Council. Some of the many awards presented to Vera in her lifetime included: the "Trailblazer Award" from The National Home Fashions League, May 1972; and the "Total Design Award" from the National Society of Interior Designers, June 1972. In addition, she was honored in 1972 with a show at the Smithsonian Institution in Washington, D.C. Vera's work has been the subject of various exhibits in the last quarter of the 20th century. She was also recently featured in the exhibit at the Museum at FIT, which is mentioned in the Tammis Keefe section above.

Pat Prichard

Pat Prichard is best known for her handkerchief designs. She also designed a wide range of household linen. In addition, she designed dinnerware and provided illustrations for print advertisements for companies such as Italian Lines. Some of her most interesting handkerchief designs are as popular among collectors as some of the better Tammis Keefe designs. However, on average, Pat Prichard handkerchiefs sell for much lower prices than handkerchiefs designed by Tammis Keefe. To date, we have not recorded prices over $50 for any of Pat Prichard's handkerchiefs. A few of her most desirable handkerchiefs including the two versions of Rich Man, Poor Man (Item 12.30) and hot-air balloon poodles (Item 14.5) sell for between $25 and $50. Her less popular designs sell for $3 and up. In a similar fashion to Tammis Keefe, Pat Prichard handkerchiefs were produced and marketed by J.H. Kimball & Company. We have included several examples of Pat Prichard's handkerchiefs with their distinctive yellow and gold J.H. Kimball & Company, Inc. paper labels in this text. Some of her handkerchief designs were repeated in scarves also bearing her signature. Pat Prichard also designed handkerchiefs for Franshaw.

In terms of household linen, Pat Prichard designed tablecloths, towels, and placemats with matching napkins. Her tablecloths and placemats are rare. Many of her towel designs are still relatively easy to find. Prices for her towels are rising; however, her tablecloths, placemats, and dinnerware can still be purchased at very reasonable prices. Prices for her towels range from $5 to $50.

To date, we have found very little written about Pat Prichard. We can say with certainty she was an active designer in the 1950s. Our collections include linen towels with her signature and 1950s copyrights. We also have a photograph of her from the magazine *Design*, Volume 58, published in 1956. Interestingly, the article was about Tammis Keefe and only mentions in passing that Pat Prichard (actually spelled Pritchard in the article) created for J. H. Kimball & Company, Inc. along with Ms. Keefe. We have not encountered anything signed by Pat Prichard dating from the 1940s or the 1960s; therefore, we are unable to say she was active in either of these two decades.

Mary Sarg

Mary Sarg, Tony Sarg's daughter, was born in 1911 in England. She studied at the Art Students League in Phoenix, Arizona and the New York School of Applied Design for Women. She was a portrait painter, teacher, and illustrator. In the 1930s she worked with her father. She became an accomplished artist on her own and her work was sold in studios in Nantucket and Florida. Her illustrations appeared in *American Girl* and *Children's Corner* in 1935, and in *Happy as a King* in 1936. She is listed in *Who Was Who in American Art*. To date we have found only one example of a textile design signed by her (Item 1.31).

Tony Sarg (1880-1942)

Tony Sarg was born in Guatemala to a German father and English mother. He spent the first six years of his life on a plantation. In 1887 the Sarg family moved to Germany where Tony was educated. He moved to England in 1905 to pursue his career as an artist. In 1909 he married and two years later Mary Eleanor Norcliffe Sarg, his only child, was born. While living in London, he had a successful career as an illustrator and commercial artist.

Fleeing the anti-German attitudes in England at the outbreak of World War I, Tony moved to America in 1915 with his wife and daughter. He rented a studio in the Flatiron Building in New York City and quickly resumed his career as an artist. His marionette hobby, which had begun when he was in England, eventually became another of his numerous professions. He became famous for his marionette making as well as for the puppet shows he staged. His company, known as Tony Sarg Marionettes, toured widely in America. In 1933, over 3 million spectators viewed puppet shows staged by his company at the Chicago World's Fair.

Tony Sarg also designed the first balloons for the Macy's Thanksgiving Day Parade in New York City in 1928. The largest of his balloons was 125 feet long. Fifty handlers were required to operate it. Huge balloons remain a tradition of the Macy's parade to this day.

One of Tony Sarg's works that is rarely mentioned was the Oasis North Lounge at The Waldorf Astoria Hotel in New York. He decorated the lounge with a wonderful mural of animals preparing and enjoying drinks. Unfortunately, this wonderful mural no longer exists.

Tony Sarg authored and illustrated numerous books, one of which is pictured in this text along with Item 5.16. He also designed cards for the National Biscuit Shredded Wheat Company. His ongoing fascination with anthropomorphic themes is very apparent in many of his book and cereal card illustrations. Pink elephants and other animals dressed in human clothing feature prominently in Tony Sarg designs.

There is limited information about Tony Sarg as a textile designer. We know he designed tablecloths, napkins, placemats, aprons, fabrics for home furnishings, and handkerchiefs. His textile designs range from fairly traditional scenes of Colonial America to outstanding anthropomorphic examples resembling those pictured in Items 5.16 and 5.18. The latter types of designs are his most collectible pieces. Prices for his napkin sets range from $25 to $125 for a set of eight. His tablecloths range in price from $75 to $150. The traditional items fall in the low range. Anthropomorphic designs like those in Items 5.16 and 5.18 are at the top of the range.

There are several examples of Tony Sarg's textile designs at the Cooper-Hewitt National Design Museum. However, they are not on permanent display and an appointment is required to see them. One of the items is very similar to the Tony Sarg apron (Item 5.16). A very interesting ink, crayon, pencil and gouache on paper by Tony Sarg is in the permanent collection at the Brandywine River Museum in Chadds Ford, Pennsylvania. The piece from 1930 is called "Laughing Lion".

Carl Tait

Carl Tait designed printed handkerchiefs, tablecloths, cocktail napkins, and towels. His handkerchiefs are difficult to find and actively pursued by collectors. All the examples we have seen with their original paper labels bear the triangular silver and black Herrmann Handkerchief Company labels. To date, we have only seen one of his designs for cocktail napkins (Item 6.17) and four tablecloth designs. Very few of his towel designs are seen in the marketplace. An example is pictured as Item 8.8.

Carl Tait's best-known handkerchief designs are from his American cities and states series. Some examples are pictured in Item 9.8. Prices for most of his handkerchiefs currently range from $15 to $60. One notable exception is his "Chicago That Wonderful Town" handkerchief, which recently sold at auction for a record $180.50.

Gustaf Tenggren (1896-1970)

Tenggren was born in the rural parish of Magda in Sweden. He studied painting from 1913-1916 at Valand, a famous art school in Sweden. From 1917 until 1926 he illustrated a popular annual of Swedish folklore and fairy tales, *Bland Tomar och Troll*. He migrated to Cleveland in 1920 and within two years he had his first art exhibit. He subsequently moved to New York where he found success as an illustrator. Between 1923 and 1939 he illustrated twenty-two books, produced product advertisements, and created romantic scenes for articles in *Good Housekeeping*, *Cosmopolitan*, *Redbook*, and *Ladies Home Journal*.

During the Great Depression, Tenggren found it difficult to make a living as a free-lance artist and he went to work for Disney in 1936. During his brief tenure at Disney Studios, he worked on *Snow White* and *Pinocchio* and various shorts including *The Ugly Duckling* and *The Old Mill*. His last assignment for the studio was *Bambi*.

Although he left Disney in 1939 and returned to illustrating children's books, his experience at Disney influenced the remainder of his career. He illustrated twenty-eight books for Golden Books between 1942 and 1962. In Tenggren's 1944 *Story Book*, he blended his old style with Disney's style. In 1956 he illustrated a cover of Walt and his Disney characters for the *Saturday Evening Post*.

Mary T. Swanson, Tenggren's biographer, describes him as "one of the most successful immigrant artists, merging a visually rich past with contemporary styles and subjects in illustrations that show a nearly seamless syntheses of old and new culture. The results can only be called 'American.' "

Rosalind Welcher

Rosalind Welcher has written and illustrated over twenty books including *The Runaway Angel*, *Social Insecurities*, *Dear Tabby*, *I Want To Be Somebody's Cat*, and *My Brother Says There's a Monster Living in Our Toilet*. Her books cover a wide range of subject matter including social commentary, humor, satire, and stories for children. She has also written, illustrated, and co-produced a children's videotape titled *When Nino Flew*. Although she has used a wide range of motifs in her work, Ms. Welcher is best known for her cat illustrations. She typically uses only her last name when signing her illustrations.

Her illustrations were used in a number of Panda Prints items including greeting cards and handkerchiefs. Several of her Panda Prints greeting cards are in the print collection of the Metropolitan Museum of Art. One example is part of the Early Twentieth Century Valentines Collection of the Museum of the City of New York. Her Chemical Bear Valentine card, c. 1950, © Panda Prints NY is pictured on the Museum of the City of New York's web site, www.mcny.org/luv.htm.

Welcher printed linen handkerchiefs are often found with their original paper labels that read "Kerchiefs by Kimball [J.H. Kimball & Company], designed by Panda Prints, Pure Linen." All the handkerchiefs that we have located with the Welcher signature have motifs for special occasions such as Christmas, Valentine's Day, and birthdays. Several other handkerchiefs in this series express sentiments such as Get Well Soon, Bon Voyage, or Thank You. Most Welcher handkerchiefs have humorous and anthropomorphic themes often featuring cats or dogs. A few depict Santa Claus, cherubs, or angels. An example of a Welcher Happy Birthday handkerchief is pictured as Item 1.28, and Item 3.12 depicts a Welcher Christmas handkerchief. Welcher handkerchiefs are currently popular with collectors and typically sell for between $12 and $35.

Bibliography

A Dictionary of Textile Terms, 14th Edition. New York, New York: Dan River Inc., 1992.

A Woman's Hand: Designing Textiles in America, 1945-69. Exhibition Brochure, The Museum at FIT, 2000.

America A to Z, Pleasantville, New York: The Reader's Digest Association, Inc., 1997.

Barr, Andrew. *Drink: A Social History of America*. New York, New York: Carroll & Graf Publishers, Inc. 1999.

Baseman, Andrew. *The Scarf*. New York, New York: Stewart, Tabori and Chang, Inc., 1989.

Canemaker, John. *Before the Animation Begins, The Art and Lives of Disney Inspirational Sketch Artists*. New York, New York: Hyperion, 1996.

Chee, Suzanne. "Tammis Keefe—A Designer During the Post-second World War Period in the United States." Master's Thesis, Fashion Institute of Technology, 1990.

Cline, D.J. *Perfection, Never Less: The Vera Way Marghab Story*. Brookings, South Dakota: South Dakota Art Museum, 1998.

Crinoline Lady in Crochet. New York, New York: The Spool Cotton Company, 1949.

Earnshaw, Pat. *The Identification of Lace*. Aylesbury, Bucks, England: Shire Publications, 1980.

Erb, Phoebe Ann. *Floral Designs from Traditional Printed Handkerchiefs*. Owings Mills, Maryland: Stemmer House Publications, Inc., 1998.

Erb, Phoebe Ann. "Get Out Your Handkerchiefs." *American Craft*, April/May 2000: 60-63, 72.

Fehling, Loretta Smith. *More Terrific Tablecloths*. Atglen, PA: Schiffer Publishing Ltd., 1999.

Fehling, Loretta Smith. *Terrific Tablecloths from the '40s and '50s*. Atglen, PA: Schiffer Publishing Ltd., 1998.

Foley, Ray. *The Ultimate Cocktail Book II*. Foley Publishing Corp., 1998.

Foster, Don. *Author Unknown*. New York, New York: Henry Holt & Company, 2000

Guild, Kathy. *Cutout Chic*. New York, New York: Garden Design, June/July 2000.

House and Garden, November 1950. The Conde Nast Publications Inc., November 1950.

Hunt, Tamara Robin. *Tony Sarg: Puppeteer in America 1915-1942*. North Vancouver, Canada: Charlemagne Press, 1988.

Husfloen, Kyle. *Black Americana Price Guide*. Dubuque, Iowa: Antique Trader Publications, 1996.

Isle, Ray. "Vintage Dish Towels." *Martha Stewart Living*, June 2001: 192-199.

Jennings, Peter, and Todd Brewster. *The Century*. New York, New York: Doubleday, 1998.

Keefe, Tammis. "Leaf (Textile Design)." *Arts and Architecture*, 1948, 65:38.

Keefe, Tammis. "The Handkerchief...Fashion Accessory." *Craft Horizons*, December 1952, 12: 24-27.

Kendall, Helen W. "Drop the Handkerchief." *Good Housekeeping*, December 1940: 190.

Kirkham, Pat, Editor. *Women Designers in the USA 1900-2000*. New Haven and London: Yale University Press, 2000.

Kurella, Elizabeth M. *Guide to Lace and Linens*. Norfolk, Virginia: Antique Trader Books, 1998.

Lambert, Eleanor. *World of Fashion*. New York, New York: R.R. Bowker Co., 1976.

Lanza, Joseph. *The Cocktail: The Influence of Spirits on the American Psyche*. New York: St. Martin's Press, 1995.

McKewen, Richard. *The Re-emergence and Re-invention of the Cocktail Way of Life*. www.nyu.edu/classes/bkg/McKewan.htm. 20 Oct. 2001.

Merz, Charles. *The Dry Decade*. Garden City, New York: Doubleday, Doran & Company, Inc., 1930.

Meserole, Mike. *20th Century Sports*. Kingston, New York: Total Sports Illustrated, 1999.

Mihalick, Roseanna. *Collecting Handkerchiefs*. Atglen, PA: Schiffer Publishing Ltd., 2000.

Moore, John Hammond. "The Cocktail: Our Contribution to Humanity's Salvation." *Virginia Quarterly Review* 56.2 (1980): 336-344.

Murphy, J.J. *Children's Handkerchiefs, A Two Hundred Year History*. Atglen, PA: Schiffer Publishing Ltd., 1998.

Neuhaus, Jessamyn. "The Way To A Man's Heart: gender roles, domestic ideology, and cookbooks in the 1950s." *Journal of Social History*, Spring 1999. www.findarticles.com/cf_0/m2005/3-32/54258700/print.jhtml.

Nissenbaum, Stephen. *The Battle for Christmas*. New York, New York: Knopf Publishing Group, 1996.

Norris, Floyd, and Christine Bockelmann. *The New York Times Century of Business*. New York, New York: McGraw-Hill, 2000.

"Only in the USA." *House & Garden*, July 1949. The Conde Nest Publications Inc. p. 32.

Opie, Iona, and Peter Opie. *The Oxford Dictionary of Nursery Rhymes, Second Edition*. Oxford, United Kingdom: Oxford University Press, 1997.

Paulson, Rose Evans. *Women's Suffrage and Prohibition: A Comparative Study of Equality and Social Control*. Glenview, Illinois: Scott, Foresman and Company, 1973.

Peri, Paolo. *The Handkerchief*. Modena, Italy: Zanfi Editori srl, 1992.

Piña, Leslie. *'50s & '60s glass, ceramic & enamel wares: designed & signed by George Briard, Sascha B., Bellaire, Higgens*. Atglen, PA: Schiffer Publishing Ltd., 1996.

"Printed In The Holiday Mood." *Design*, 1956, 58: 65-66.

Rachowiecki, Rob. *Southwest*. Melbourne, Oakland, London, Paris: Lonely Planet Publications,1999.

Scofield, Elizabeth, and Peggy Zalamea,. *20th Century Linens and Lace, A Guide to Identification, Care, and Prices of Household Linens*. Atglen, PA: Schiffer Publishing Ltd., 1995.

Shaw, Josephine. *The Hostess's Complete Handbook*. New York, New York: The Homemaker's Encyclopedia, Inc., 1952.

"The Hand and the Handle." *Arts & Architecture* 1965, 65: 24-27.

Thomas, Mary. *Mary Thomas' Dictionary of Embroidery Stitches*. New York: Gramercy Park Publishing Company, 1935.

Walker, Carolyn, and Kathy Holman. *The Embroidery of Madeira*. New York, New York: Union Square Press, 1987.

Walker, Stanley. *The Night Club Era*. New York City: Blue Ribbon Books, Inc. 1933.

Who Was Who in American Art: 1564-1975. Madison, Connecticut: Sound View Press, 1999, I:223; III, 2891.

Zimmerman, Nancy. *American Southwest*. Hong Kong: Twin Age Ltd., 2001.

Index